CHALK TALK

A SURVIVAL GUIDE FOR BEGINNING EDUCATORS

2nd Edition

Judy Jackson May

Bowling Green State University

Todd R Edmond

Tiffin City Schools

Linus
Publications, Inc.

Published by Linus Publications, Inc.
Deer Park, NY 11729

ISBN 10: 1-60797-261-1

ISBN 13: 978-1-60797-261-7

Printed in the United States of America.

This book is printed on acid-free paper.

Print Numbers   5   4   3   2   1

Dedication

To my wife and three children – my strength and my life. To my father and mother – who always believed in me, and taught me to believe in myself. To my brothers, whom I've always looked up to (both figuratively, and literally). To my students - who, day after day, continue to teach *me* as much as I teach *them*.

~Todd R Edmond

This book is dedicated to my parents Carlos Anderson Jackson (1930-1974) and Dr. Faith Lilly Jackson, who gave of themselves to put the world at my feet. And to my blessed children, Jennifer Erin, Jacquelyn Elyse, and Alicia Anne, without whose unconditional love, support and devotion I would cease to be.

~Judy Jackson May

Table of Contents

Acknowledgements

This practical book was borne from the discussions of two educators searching to find a text to fit the needs of preservice teachers. From a teacher who developed a novice teacher handbook, and a professor who saw the promise and possibilities emerged this handy little guide.

Todd Edmond would like to thank the guidance and support shown by Dr. Diane Armstrong, Dr. Denise Callihan, Mr. Joe Moore, the Heidelberg College Education Department, and fellow teachers (and brothers), Mr. Tim Edmond and Mr. Ted Edmond – who paved the way for brother number three to enter the education field.

Dr. May would like to acknowledge the support of her friends and colleagues Dr. Patrick D. Pauken, Dr. Mychail B. Scheramic, Mrs. Vickie Digby, Dr. W. Kyle Ingle, Dr. Eric D. Myers, Dr. Paul Johnson, Dr. Judith Zimmerman, Dr. Craig Mertler, Dr. Adrienne Noel, and Dr. Eugene T.W. Sanders. She would also like to express sincere love and appreciation to her sister, Patricia Jackson Nevils, who has been her constant companion on this journey called life; Chiann Elyse May, who makes being Nana the greatest profession on Earth; and to Adam Dunn, a summer 2007; EDAS 409 student who taught her that wisdom comes in unsuspecting packages. Much appreciation is extended to the hundreds of preservice teachers who have enriched her both professionally and personally over the past thirteen years.

This project was richly enhanced by the many students who freely contributed their case stories. They are a bold and proud reminder of the success of teacher education programs:

Carissa Smith is a 4th grade teacher at Raphael Catholic School in Raleigh North Carolina

Aaron Turner is a 2nd grade teacher at Johnsville Elementary School in Northmor Local, Ohio

Kathy Solomon is a 3rd grade teacher as Golbow Elementary in Katy Independent School District, Houston, Texas

Jennifer Erin May is a secondary Language Arts teacher at Max Hayes Vocational School in the Cleveland Metropolitan Schools, Cleveland, Ohio

Gereon Vaughn Methner is a secondary French teacher in Shawano Community Schools, Shawano, Wisconsin

Jennifer Wancata is a kindergarten teacher in the Chicago Public Schools

Jacquelyn May is a secondary history and economics teacher at Prepa Tec Valle Alto of Tecnologico de Monterrey, Nuevo Leon, Mexico.

Chad Warnimont is a 5th grade teacher at Toth Elementary School in Perrysburg, Ohio

Larry Kisabeth is the Principal at Tiffin Columbian High School in Tiffin, Ohio

With special thanks to Amy Laukhuf-Fitch, M. Ed, who graciously and expertly edited each chapter with care while teaching language arts for Otsego Local Schools.

Preface

Thousands of novice educators enthusiastically enter the teaching profession in the United States each year. Some choose to begin their careers in rural schools; some choose suburban environments and others select urban settings. While the demographics of each school may vary, the fundamental skills necessary for teacher success remain constant. Students require educators who are engaged, knowledgeable, forward thinking, adaptable, and reflective. *Chalk Talk: A Survival Guide for Beginning Educators* is designed to be a practical approach to preparing 21st century teachers. To compliment the courses in teacher preparation programs, this text judiciously presents a selection of core topics necessary to carry a novice teacher into their first classroom.

Informed by the authors' 40 years of combined educational experience, the text addresses new teacher skills in a realistic context for functional application. Utilizing the writings, research, and experience of experts in the field, this book is designed to be a relevant reference guide during the first year of teaching. *Chalk Talk* can assist in providing a solid foundation in the professional growth process of novice teachers.

Overview of the Book

The book is organized into 9 practical chapters. All but three begin with an actual case story from a practicing novice educator. We gathered a variety of case stories representing a wide spectrum of schools and teachers. The stories are from teachers in parochial, rural, urban, suburban, and international schools. Each chapter ends with skill building activities to assist in applying the material to practical situations.

Chapter one discusses securing the first teaching position, from choosing the district that is the right fit, to resume writing to getting through the actual interview. The chapter also offers tips for the novice teacher with regard to additional duties and life beyond the school day.

The second chapter provides a perspective on teacher professionalism, school district organization, and how to build collegial relationships.

Chapter three illustrates how philosophy and history inform classroom instructional practices.

Chapter four assists novice teachers in creating a well-managed classroom. The information is presented in a clear understandable format for teachers of all levels.

Chapter five and six provide a clear perspective on the basics of school law and finance for novice teachers.

A discussion on accountability and standards is presented in chapter seven and chapter eight and chapter nine address instructing culturally diverse classrooms and exceptional children respectively.

YOU'VE RADUATED! NOW WHAT?

THE INTERVIEW

Carissa Smith is a fourth grade teacher at Raphael Catholic School in Raleigh North Carolina and this is her story.

I knew I wanted to be a teacher since third grade. The day I graduated from college, I was so proud of myself. As I received my diploma, I was determined to be the best teacher anyone had ever seen. But......I needed a job.

That's where the fun began. In the months that followed graduation, I sent out resumes on a daily basis. I spent hours on the computer looking up school districts for what positions were available. Not many. I knew this would be hard. I remembered one of my favorite professors telling me, "It's going to be hard for you to get a job right now. You have to make your resume different from everyone else's. You have to "stand out." Stand out, I thought. I graduated from one of the best teaching colleges in the nation, and had a perfect GPA, and was involved in many different professional organizations, campus activities, and community service. Wasn't that enough?

Sending out resumes wasn't enough. So I would call schools every day to "check up" on my file so that they knew I was interested. But, every time, the response remained the same: "I'm sorry, we don't have any positions available at this time." Or else I would get a letter in the mail saying that the school would keep my resume on file, but nothing was open. What was I going to do? I had to get a job. After all, this is what I went to college for!

Then-I got the call. Finally! A principal from a city two hours away called to say that he had just had a teacher decide to retire and they needed someone to take her place; in kindergarten! I knew that might be hard, but I was as excited as anything! I drove to the interview as nervous as could be. The principal, Mr. Johnson, was very nice; a tall, dark haired man that looked to be in his 40s. He was easy to talk to and made me feel more comfortable. He asked me all sorts of questions and to each one, I replied honestly, giving specific examples from my limited experience to back up what I was saying. After I left, I looked at the clock and realized I'd been interviewing for over an hour and a half. Well then, I thought to myself, he must have liked me! In my head I started to critique all the things that I had done wrong or could have done better. I disliked leaving the interview not knowing whether I would get this job or not.

One day passed, two days passed, three days passed. I've got to call him back, I thought. So with a knot in my throat, a pit in my stomach and sweaty palms, I began to dial. He answered. I nervously told him who I was and asked, "I was wondering where you are in the hiring process?" A pause. The knot in my throat suddenly began to cut off my air supply and I felt faint. "Well, Miss Smith…" he began. "After receiving over 70 resumes for this position and interviewing 10 people, it was down to you and one other lady. You see, this other lady has five years of experience…." He quickly added, "And I really like you, Miss Smith. I just think that the parents at this school will feel more comfortable having a teacher with some experience in kindergarten." I was mortified. "But" he continued. "I just got off the phone with a principal right down the road. She is looking for some new energy and I gave you a really good recommendation. She needs a second grade teacher and is still in the building if you'd like to give her a call."

Carissa's story is not atypical and most times securing that first job requires some real know-how. Chapter one provides what you will need to make that first teaching position a reality.

CONGRATULATIONS! You are now licensed educator! You know all there is to know about education-from books anyway. Now you have the most difficult task of deciding where to go from here. You will join the ranks of 150,000 teacher graduates who will be embarking on the same challenges as you.[1] But don't fret as you can take comfort in the knowledge that you have chosen a most noble and rewarding profession. There are nearly 3.2 million public school teachers in the United States [2] and contrary to what you may have heard over 80% of them are satisfied with their profession and would choose to pursue the path all over again [3].

This journey begins before you even reach college. Each year over 3 million high school seniors graduate into the real world.[2] Their faces bring back memories of how graduation feels; both in high school and college. The sense of accomplishment. The sense of confidence in reaching a major milestone in life. And, of course, total fear and panic.

More so than high school, college graduation day is a day filled with joy and irony. The same institution that told you to have pride and self-determination now cuts you loose to fend for yourself with that wonderful piece of paper in hand that tells the world that you are "ready!" Graduation is a wonder of all wonders. We all can relate vividly to the commencement speaker whose 45-minute speech on *Computers in the Workplace* did not provide many answers. Nor did the fellow classmate recovering from a drunken stupor the night before have any professional insight to offer. All of a sudden, you can feel very alone in the world. So if fear is what you are feeling, do not worry, it is a normal part of the process!

So, for many of you the first thought is to run home for advice. Luckily, many of you, much like other teacher graduates, have relatives who are educators. They may be a great help in providing the frame of mind to begin hunting for work. Assistance may come from a family member, but it also may come from your old school counselor or a cooperating teacher under whom you trained. More than likely, there is someone out there somewhere you can trust. Find that person and tap them for information on getting that first classroom. Nine times out of ten, they will be able to share some tid-bit of information that assists in your journey. The college placement office may be willing to help also, but you may find your relatives more "in the know" since they are actually practicing in the field that you are entering.

The old adage "It's not *what* you know, but *who* you know" is so true. And in fact over 40% of teachers secure their teaching positions through a "back door" of which other candidates are unaware.[4] So use the contacts you have made to your advantage.

Interviewing

If you are like most college graduates, you probably were briefed on what to expect from a job interview. Maybe you even had the opportunity to participate in a few mock interviews. If so, then you have a good base from which to draw confidence. As mentioned, colleges and universities have offices dedicated to assisting students as they embark on their first quest for a teaching position. It is wise to check out the free services available to you at your current institution. There may be printed materials, audio-visual aides, and personnel to assist in the process.

Whether it is an on-campus, on-site, or a telephone interview, the first step to a successful exchange is preparation. Interview preparation includes knowing yourself, knowing the district, practicing your responses, carrying a winning attitude, and being aware of your non-verbal communication.[5]

What to know and do

Knowing yourself includes the ability to effectively describe your skills, interests and work values as well as identifying strengths and weaknesses. Additionally, you should be able to discuss in a two-minute speech, your long and short term goals, examples illustrating the development of your skill, key accomplishments, key items on your resume, and why you are interested in the position.

Knowing the district requires you to have consulted any number of resources such as the district web site, State Report Card, annual reports, newspapers, and personnel currently employed in district if possible. You should be familiar with the district's mission statement, goals, core values, organizational structure, recent significant events, statewide academic standing, results of the most recent annual testing in your subject area, and the district's academic strengths and weaknesses.

A winning attitude is the most significant tool you can take to your interview. All the skills, know-how, and training in the world cannot overcome

a poor attitude. This is what the interview team will most remember when you have departed. Leave them to remember that you were enthusiastic, prepared, demonstrated a positive demeanor, and presented yourself as one who will be committed to the goals of the district.

Purdue University Center for Career Opportunities suggests adhering toa few general rules stressing the importance of professional dress, impeccable grooming and the absence of scents and perfumes.[6] Professional dress for both men and women includes a suit with matching shoes of reasonable height minimizing all jewelry and adornments. The Center also recommends the interviewee greet with a firm, but not overpowering handshake that meets"web to web." Eye contact should be maintained from the beginning to the end of the interview, avoiding the urge to look at the wall or floor. While gestures are a necessary and normal part of conversation, movements should not become the focal point. Lastly, interviewee should be mindful of posture: be comfortable without slouching or appearing mechanical.

Speaking of non-verbals

Your nonverbal body communication forms the first impression the prospective employer gathers of you and there are no "do-overs." These impressions are formed from your handshake, eye contact, grooming, gestures and posture. Researchers note that the impact of your nonverbal cues may override your verbal communication performance. Eugene Raudsepp of the College Journal writes that only 7% of the messages and perceptions you send are gathered through spoken language. Fifty–five percent of your messages emanate through your body language and 38% through your use of voice.[7]

The process

The interview process can be best described as having three stages; establishing rapport, gathering information and closing the interview.[5] Establishing rapport begins with the first impression, which can be neither understated nor re-established once done. Your rapport is established in the first few seconds through your initial responses, tone, and physical appearance. While the interview team is gathering information about your qualifications it is essential that you provide concrete examples that illustrate how your experiences, skills, and training are a good fit with their district. When closing the interview you will typically be provided the opportunity to ask questions. Make sure you have some questions prepared which may include inquiries about the position, organization, selection process, and time-line for follow-up.

While the interview practices outlined here may be typical, the bottom line is that no two interviews are alike-even in the same district. It all depends on who is asking the questions and what the district is seeking in a new teacher.

Don't concern yourself with who you are replacing or if it is a new position. Either way it will not affect your interview performance. So don't waste time worrying about it.

The following five points provide guidance in the interview preparation process.

1. *Develop an impressive, but simple resume.* Never use a book when a chapter will do. Assume that the prospective employer has a dozen people to consider for a position and needs to learn as much information about you from the resume in as little time as possible. If they want to know that your favorite hobby is dog grooming, please know, they'll ask. Otherwise, it's a good idea to keep your resume to one page. A sample resume is provided in the appendix.

2. *Develop a well written cover letter.* A cover letter, along with the application and resume is often the "first real look" the district will have of you. It should move them to want to "learn" more about you by exploring your other materials. A poorly written cover letter may negatively impact your chances of securing an interview. The purpose of the cover letter is to gain information about a position (letter of inquiry) or to declare your desire for a position (letter of application). A cover letter is typically three paragraphs in length and (1) describes the position for which you are applying, (b)

highlights your academic qualifications, skills, experiences, and personal attributes and (c) describes some course of action to be considered. A sample cover letter is provided in the appendix.

3. *Develop a portfolio.* It is always helpful to have examples of your teaching style ready to show a prospective employer. Worksheets, tests, unit plans and even lesson plans from your student teaching days will go a long way in helping the school system figure out what kind of educator you can be. Often, an employer will ask you about your educational philosophy. An educational philosophy is a well constructed document that provides a snapshot of your educational belief systems, philosophical school of thought, teaching style and approaches to classroom management. A sample educational philosophy appears in the appendix. Having these items handy may assist in your responses.

    A CD-rom with information about yourself and your teaching style can also be very helpful and impressive-but make sure you have multiple copies since most employers will not want to take time away from the interview to view what you have prepared. More often than not, schools will ask you to describe your teaching style, or maybe even teach a section of a lesson to them. Having a portfolio ready will show not only your preparedness, but also your professionalism and organizational skills as well.

4. *Dress for success!* It goes without saying that your attire will be a significant part of the first impression any employer forms. As previously noted there is only one chance to make a first impression. Look your best. Look professional. Leave the torn, worn, tired-looking shirt, pants, and shoes in your closet. If money is tight, it is advisable is to purchase one "interview outfit" and wear it for nothing else. Always have it pressed and ready to go–you never know when you will only have 20 minutes to get to that interview for which you have been waiting. This is hardly enough time to get dressed; let alone wash, dry and iron! So be ready at a moment's notice.

5. *Arrive 15 minutes early.* No employer wants to wait for you. Arrive at the interview early and be ready the moment they want to see you. You will be surprised how a little adjustment time will set the pace for a positive interview. An early arrival also signals to a prospective employer that you want the job and are responsible enough to get to work on time. You can never get there too early, but one minute too late is one minute too many!

6. *Try to relax, but realize that nerves are part of the game.* Don't worry about showing up nervous. A cold or sweaty handshake is normal and the employer is probably used to it. Actually, nerves sometime show an employer how much you really want the job. The jitters typically dissipate after the first few questions are asked. Just take a deep breath, have confidence in yourself and answer each question honestly. Honesty is always the best policy.

Just remember, the confidence you have in yourself will pour out in the interview-you don't even have to try to do it, it will just happen on its own. Use the following steps to prepare yourself and only worry about what *you* can control. Good luck!

CHOOSING A JOB

During your senior year you may have been warned by college personnel about the availability of teaching positions in your area, or more specifically what positions WERE NOT available. Over the last decade the number of public elementary and secondary school teachers has risen faster than the number of students,[8] but there are still plenty of positions out there. However, the news is both good and bad. Even though the days of hearing about teacher oversupply appear to have ebbed, there are still geographic locations and subject areas that are more and less desirable. While there are exceptions to every rule, trends show that demand is highest in urban, west and southwestern areas and lower in the Middle Atlantic, Great Lakes, and Northeastern areas. Bilingual education, math, science, computer science, and special education continue to be subjects of high demand [2] whereas there is less demand for social studies and language arts. In recent years baby boomers have begun to retire creating an abundance of teaching positions all across the nation. Additionally, Senate Bill 55 provides some districts increased flexibility to lower class sizes; which, in turn, means the possibility of adding more teachers to teach more classes. So, for example, a history class of 32 now becomes two classes of 16. More and more graduates are able to choose where they want to teach, rather than the jobs choosing them. Some systems in the west are even offering signing bonuses to attract teachers. Las Vegas for example reportedly not only offers signing bonuses, but covers travel to the state for the interview and moving expenses as well. When it comes to finding the job that you want, several factors will more than likely play into your decision. It could range from salary to family to, yes, even a "significant other." When you search for a job, try not to let money lead you. While the dollars you make dictate your lifestyle, the bottom line is that if you take a job for money it may not prove to be the most personally satisfying position. You hopefully didn't choose the teaching profession with the idea of becoming rich-if you did, someone has played a cruel joke on you! So when you choose a job, keep money in mind, but don't use it as your guide.

Variables to Consider

According to the United States Department of Labor the median annual income for teachers in the United States is $47, 674 with the lowest 10% earning $28, 590 to $33, 070 and the top 10% earning $67,490 to $76,100.[9] Luckily, financial compensation does not appear to weigh in heavily in the job selection process as two-thirds of the nation's first year teachers don't perceive the financial compensation as a drawback.[8]

There are many other variables to consider that may outweigh the financial compensation, such as the culture of the community and what will be expected of you in the teaching position. For instance, what is the belief system of the school? What is the socioeconomic makeup? What is the culture of the community? What is the racial makeup of the school system? And of course look at what classes you will be expected to teach and whether you are comfortable teaching them. You may also ask for a copy of the course curriculum, texts and any supplemental materials at your disposal. A quick review of these documents may answer some of your questions. In addition, if you are secondary, make sure to ask how many preps you will be expected to teach. There are too many harrowing stories about new teachers who sign on for five or more new preps a day and find themselves struggling to stay afloat. All in all, when choosing a system find out about the qualities that are important to you. Avoid accepting an unattractive assignment assuming it will be just be a "stepping stone." It may wind up being the system from which you retire! So choose wisely and have a list of priorities to guide you in making a sound decision for yourself.

While money shouldn't be the driving force, remember to at least ask or look into the financial stability of the system and the community. If you see factories or major stores leaving the area, that is not the best sign for the local tax base of the school system. On the other hand, if the Ford Motor Company has its headquarters in town, you're in good hands. One way to look into a town's finances is to sometimes just ask the local people. Go into the barbershop, bakery or grocery store and listen to what is being said. Drive around the area and look for new stores or factory life that exists. Read the local paper editorials and try to get a feel for the mood of the town. Another district financial indicator is the school's technological pursuits. Ask to see the computer lab in the school district to see if the computers are new or old, and how many will be accessible to you and your students. If a school has outdated computers, or has never heard of a "Smart Board," they may not have the funding to update their technology systems.

It's all about the benefits

One last, but certainly not least, variable to remember when choosing your school system is the benefits package offered. Medical costs are skyrocketing at a rate of about 25% per year. What you need to know is how much your out-of-pocket costs will be for medical, dental and vision insurance, for single and family coverage. When you factor in the costs of insurance many experienced teachers will tell you that the benefits package far outweighs what appears to be a lower salary.

When examining the benefits package it is important understand what options may be available to you. One is the "cafeteria plan" where, much like a food line, you choose what services you want covered. Other systems have a consortium where the medical care providers are part of a plan that has negotiated rates with certain procedures and certain doctors in the area. If this plan is in your system, you need to review the list of "in-network" doctors and "out-of-network" doctors. The out-of-network doctors may still be covered for some procedures with additional out-of-pocket expense. This becomes an issue if you have specific medical concerns.

Along with medical insurance new teachers must also consider the investment and retirement opportunities. Careful and thoughtful financial planning is essential for educators. Most, if not all, school systems offer some type of structured retirement plan such as the State Teachers Retirement System (STRS). STRS is a mandatory retirement system where a portion of your income is deducted and combined with a district contribution. These funds are invested on your behalf and are not accessible until retirement. But it is essential that you also do some personal planning in order to maximize your retirement income. Some districts also offer 401k, 403b, and 457b plans. In these optional individual retirement accounts (IRA) you can save and invest money before it is taxed. Thus, if you decide to invest in some other kind of retirement plan, you are not penalized for the money you withhold and invest. A word of caution if you decide to invest: do your homework prior to investing out your hard-earned dollars. Some school systems hire an investment firm to provide advice. It is still wise to seek a second opinion and know what you want going into the process. The good news is, the sooner you begin planning, saving, and investing, the more time the money will have to grow on your behalf. Just make sure you are aware that any investment is a gamble. Risk is always a part of the game.

Once you are hired in your teaching position employers should review the benefit package with you. Be sure to bring this up when they ask you if you have any questions. Again, the salary schedule is important, but the benefit package is equally vital.

And finally, you have graduated, searched, applied, interviewed, and received the ultimate reward: a job offer. Now, one of the last, but most exciting, activities in which you will engage is the signing of your contract. The contract represents a binding agreement between you and the school district. It establishes your conditions of work, general duties, and your salary and benefits. Until you earn the security of a continuing contract, known as tenure, your contract is renewed each year. While most novice teacher contracts are fairly standard, it is wise to take the time to read it over carefully.

A Real-World Perspective

The beginning of the chapter provided a job search perspective from a practicing novice teacher. There will be opportunities throughout this book to hear from a variety of individuals who are living what is written in these pages. Below you will read from someone who sits on the other side of the table; the interviewer. Reading these words of wisdom may serve as an invaluable resource for you as you begin your quest for your first professional post.

THE INTERVIEW

Larry Kisabeth is a principal at Tiffin Columbian High School in Tiffin, Ohio and he offers a unique perspective on the interview process.

The interviewing process is a good process to go through. It can be very nerve wracking for a young person, but the more one interviews, the better he/she will become.

The resume should be one or, at the most, two pages in length. It should be neat and concise so it may be scanned quickly for pertinent information. The names of references complete with phone numbers are very important. Once we select our finalists we will call references first. If possible, list those who know you in different roles in your life.

Many candidates will bring in portfolios for review-then be disappointed if they are not used. The portfolio is an important document, but I believe it is more important to the interviewee than the interviewer. The interviewee benefits from the portfolio because it forces the candidate to organize his/her philosophy and beliefs on paper. By working through a portfolio, the candidate is able to explore and confirm what he/she really believes.

Meanwhile, the interviewer may scan the portfolio to examine the quality and the organization of the document. He may also read letters of reference. However, the interviewer will not spend a great amount of time reviewing the portfolio.

Overall, the interview process is an important one. When looking at a person for a teaching position, the process tends to be a two-way street. This must be a good fit for all parties involved for a good marriage between the candidate and the position. The interviewer must be comfortable and confident in the candidate. The same, meanwhile, must be true for the candidate. If either is not, then the hiring process should not take place.

When a candidate is not hired for a position, any disappointment should be short-lived. Keep in mind the hiring process must be a "win-win" situation for all involved.

All I ever needed to know about teaching, I learned in college: But... little advice won't hurt

As you move closer to your very first classroom and your first day as a teacher it is exciting to think about *finally* being able to use what you have learned. This section offers some recommendations to increase the likelihood of a smooth transition to a teaching career.

The "Professional's Lounge"

The teacher's lounge is a topic that many of you will or have experienced during student teaching. The Lounge (notice the capital letter - due to the fact that it really is an establishment - much like a bar or pub) is a place where new teachers may become disillusioned in one way or another. It can be a cauldron for bad attitudes, stories, disasters, and bad jokes. A word of advice for new teachers is to avoid burned-out teachers who want to vent about every class. Good judgment and common sense is the best guide. Some of the best friends in the education world may have been in the business for decades. Likewise, some of the biggest complainers may be the youngest teachers. The Lounge is meant to be a reprieve, a relaxation getaway inside the walls of the school where a teacher can have a snack or a drink (water or pop!) and escape the teaching world for a short while. Avoid talking about school while in the lounge. If people are persistent about focusing on negativity, first try to change the subject, if that is unsuccessful try to find a more relaxing location to spend a few minutes.

In the early years of teaching, it is of the utmost importance to create a circle of positive people. Too many young teachers are drawn into "pity parties" (for lack of a better term) by burned-out educators who tell them, "I'm sure glad I don't have twenty-nine more years in this profession!" This is talk you really do not need. Find the enthusiastic teachers who have fun in the classroom, the teachers who are driven to enjoy life and to help students. "The Lounge" can be a great place of relaxation and conversation, and as long as it stays positive, enjoy it. When the "dark side" surfaces, leave as fast as you can! There are enough instigators of burnout. Don't let the Lounge become one of them.

Endless Sea of Papers

Paperwork is often one part of teaching that no one enjoys. The seemingly endless sea of papers that flow between mailboxes can be overwhelming. As mentioned earlier, effective organization can assist in keeping track of the tome of necessary paperwork. Outside the typical paperwork, the most time-consuming "assignment" will be preparing lesson plans. Lesson plans are required by many districts as a way to document what is being taught, when it is being taught, and how it is being taught. While some teachers take a negative view of lesson plans, try to see the bright side. Lesson plans provide building administrators an opportunity to take a brief look inside the classroom process.

Administrators may not have time to stop by teacher's classrooms regularly. There might be a great classroom project coming up that they would like to witness, but would not know about unless you provided the lesson plans for review. Lesson plans keep the administrators and teachers on the same page. While paranoid teachers may say lesson plans are a way for the administration to spy, the truth is, administrators should know everything you are teaching to students. Teachers who have an open door at all times have nothing to hide. It worries good teachers and administrators, when educators repudiate turning in lesson plans; it may signal that something in the classroom may not be quite right.

While lesson plans are a great way to keep the administrators abreast of your daily activities, plans can also be a helpful tool to plan ahead. Too many teachers claim they don't have enough time to cover all the material in the curriculum. Some teachers are weeks behind on a project because they have not taken the opportunity to look into the future and budget their time wisely. Lesson plans and a calendar are fundamental when setting up the term or, or even the entire school year. It's very similar to planning a personal budget. The difference between what comes in and goes out is your "playtime" fund.

Naturally, "play money" would never be taken out before all the bills are paid. Likewise, classroom instruction should begin with what must be covered first.

In order to make the first semester flow more smoothly, some schools are now deciding to make first semester final exams occur before the winter break instead of the usual mid-January. Those schools feel that students should be able to enjoy break and come back ready to go for a new semester. The drawback this format creates is unbalanced semesters. The first semester is sixteen weeks long, while the second semester takes up twenty weeks. In a year-round class it's no problem, but when teaching a semester class, creative planning is a must. All in all, lesson plans are a great way to ease your mind, mapping out curricular expectations. Many teachers end up taking the extra couple of weeks in the spring and incorporating a wonderful class project where they explore the interests of their students. This is not as feasible during the first semester because all sixteen weeks are needed for instruction. Appropriate and thoughtful planning is crucial for teachers to complete the curriculum requirements on time. In this era of standardized assessments, it is the duty of all educators to make sure the evaluated material is covered in the classroom.

Aside from lesson plans, the other paperwork encountered on a daily basis can be anything from attendance, to sub folders, to National Society forms. The key is to make sure to stay on top of it. Do not let papers pile up on the desk. This will only create frustration. Instead, complete them as soon as possible. Organization is the key to sound classroom.

Life after 4:00 p.m.

Almost every teacher that comes into the profession faces an "alternate agenda" of after-school activities. There are limitless opportunities to become involved in school related activities beyond the school day. The source of these events could come from academic activities, sports, clubs or other groups related to the school district. The accountability measures mandated by the No Child Left Behind Act of 2001 provide many tutoring and supplemental service opportunities for teachers beyond the school day. Many new teachers may assume that extracurricular activities are part of educator's job, and they are willing to be active participants. While these activities are not necessarily part of the job description, they do provide fun and satisfying opportunities to further your involvement with your students, school, and community.

Often times, new teachers are not aware of the time commitment involved or the challenges presented with additional duties. Some additional responsibilities are paid and some are not. Compensated activities are called "supplemental contracts" and are issued to teachers performing duties that are *in addition* to the regular teaching day. Many states have laws requiring written contracts for these extra responsibilities as delineated in the state's Revised Code.[10] These contracts can be quite lucrative, but it is important that new teachers carefully weigh the benefits as well as the drawbacks. This section will discuss the responsibilities connected with these activities.

EXTRACURRICULAR SCHOOL ACTIVITIES

Coaching

Many educators are drawn to teaching for the classroom as well as the opportunity to teach through coaching outside the classroom. Maybe it is a return to past glory or a desire to compete, but whatever the reason, the new coach should know what is in store before the post is accepted.

One pleasure of coaching is having a group of players to call your own. If you were an athlete in your younger days, you view the game from the perspective of a *member* of the team. As a coach, however, you are now *in charge* of leading the team. A big difference! As a coach, you extend your classroom role and become a role model and a builder of moral character outside the classroom as well. It is a big job, but there are some tips to guide you to a fun and satisfying experience.

Coaches must be organized - plain and simple. An unorganized coach will lose his players within a matter of weeks. It is a lot like teaching. If your room is unorganized, kids notice and may not be motivated to perform to their capabilities. Likewise, if your practice sessions have no focus, or simply do not start on time, your players will perform at the same level.

The hours and effort of preparation is usually what determine whether the team, and ultimately you, is successful. It begins with you - the leader. The coach's main job is to set the tone of the group. If you are unorganized and slow to react or plan, the season will be over before it begins.

One good idea is to keep a separate bag or briefcase for your sport. This is important for two reasons. One, your material will be in one location and not lost with other school paperwork. This will eliminate having to search for practice plans, physical cards, and other information that may be mixed in with teaching material. A separate bag or folder for these materials will go a long way in preventing headaches for you.

In addition to separating materials for organizational reasons, it is wise to do so for teaching reasons as well. Remember, when you are at school during the day you are a teacher first, and a coach second. The focus on academics is vital. Do not cheat the students or yourself by reducing academics for extra curricular activities. Be aware that students do notice when their teacher is *not* attending to the class.

Keep in mind that 95% of the money you take home is for educating students, not coaching. The students in your classroom are the main focus of your job. Athletics and extracurricular activities are just that: *Extra*curricular. Keep your focus on the task at hand and you will do fine.

Parents & Coaching

Remember that behind every athlete is a parent; one who believes his or her little cherub is a "star." The following is a reality check for dealing with parents.

At some point in your coaching career, you will probably hear the following come from parents:

"Why did you cut my son? He made the Babe Ruth All-Stars two years in a row."

"She's been in gymnastics since she was 3."

"Where did you learn to coach? You obviously never played the sport before!"

"I was a star volleyball player when I was here and she's better than me!"

"Hey coach, play the bench kids, they should be starting anyway!"

Although most parents are great supporters, some can be a challenge. The key to dealing with those challenges is to remember that each parent feels his or her kid is the next Alex Rodriguez, LeBron James, Peyton Manning, Gabrielle Reece, or Mia Hamm. The parents' view of their child's abilities will always be subjective. As the coach, your job is to listen to parent concerns and validate them. Responding angrily to concerned parents will only serve to exacerbate an already tense situation.

Understand that it is vital that you communicate with parents. However, when faced with an upset parent, the best way to deal with the situation is to *listen* without becoming defensive. You will be surprised how quickly the emotions will calm down. Be supportive, but also quiet. Let parents vent and they will feel better.

While the doom and gloom surrounding parents may seem to be at the forefront, do not fret as those same parents will also be your biggest support group during the season. Think of it this way: when you were growing up your parents were more than likely your biggest fans. They attended and supported all your extracurricular interests. Some of you even had parents who were able to fork out hundreds of dollars in music lessons, football, baseball, hockey, and soccer equipment, dance lessons, swim lessons and the list goes on and on. Your parents were always there when you needed support for a new "project." Your student-athletes have parents who feel the same way. Those same parents will in turn support you as their kid's coach. They may offer unsolicited advice, but at the end they will be the rock upon which your team depends. During your coaching years your team's parents will be at every game - win or lose - offering smiles, cheers, and sometimes post-game meals. Never will they waiver in their devotion to the program. You may even have a parent bring a gas grill to a doubleheader soccer match and make hamburgers and hot dogs for BOTH teams between games. Really, it happens!

Parents who care are what we strive for in education. Coaches need to encourage parents to get involved with the program. You can do this by offering ways parents can help - such as selling tickets, working the concession stand, announcing, singing the national anthem, and making programs. Parents who become active in their kid's life will positively influence the group as a whole.

Try to remember that school athletics are not meant for a "win at all costs" mentality. A coach's job at this level is to teach kids how to play together as a team, and how to rely on someone else, no matter what special gifts they may possess as an individual. The competition on the field should nurture a sense of teamwork and sportsmanship. Think back to your own days as a player. Try to remember, without thinking of wins or losses, what you liked and disliked about the program. Build on the positives while learning from the unpleasant moments.

AN AUTHOR CASE STORY:

The greatest rule of thumb anyone ever told me in regarding coaching came from my Dad - who was a high school sports writer for over 30 years. He said, "Don't dwell on the scoreboard too much. In ten years, you won't know what record your team had; but what you will know are the players and memories of being a part of that team."

You know what? He was right.

Clubs

If coaching is not up your alley, or if you are a workaholic who just needs to fill those extra couple of hours each week, being a club advisor might be for you!

As you probably know, schools are great at creating a club for virtually every kind of student. Language clubs (Spanish, French), athletic clubs (Wrestling, Ski), special interest clubs (SADD), religious clubs (STAND), academic clubs (Quiz Bowl, Science Club) and so on. These clubs offer a great way to see your students in another environment. It can offer great insight as to just what goes on in their minds!

When you sign up for an advisory position, do not let money be a factor because the pay is often minimal. Join a group for the same reason as the kids – interest, adventure, and fun. Clubs offer a great way to teach without the bell, homework, or lesson plan demands of the regular classroom. You will be amazed what you will learn from just sitting on a bench eating lunch with a bunch of teenagers on a Saturday afternoon. It offers great insight into their world.

At the same time, you are learning about your students, they are also learning more about you. As an advisor, you are showing students how much they actually matter to you outside of what grade they are earning in your class. For some of the kids, your club may be the best part of their week or even their school year.

Clubs may be much work for the advisor - planning activities, being the "responsible adult," emergency medical forms, parent phone calls, and the list goes on. While the work can be long and sometimes challenging, the personal reward is worth far more than monetary gain.

Most schools have a "get involved" motto for their students. Keep in mind that the same rule applies to you as a teacher. The more involved you become, the better educator you will be. So do not be shy, be ready to help any way you can. It will only make you a stronger teacher in the end.

AN AUTHOR CASE STORY:

I started a "History Club" at Tiffin Columbian High School. Over the years, we have taken weekend trips to historical sites around our area. The most notable accomplishment to date was being a part of the Civil War excavation at Johnson's Island near Marblehead, Ohio. We teamed up with Heidelberg College's Archeology Department, who graciously allowed us to work alongside them for a hands-on experience into the Civil War era.

I receive no pay. Yep, NO pay, for being the club's advisor. I would not have it any other way. Money is not the issue when dealing with kids on this level. I have a first hand opportunity to watch them experiencing learning and growing. The discovery and excitement of the group are what drive me to continue as their advisor.

A few years ago, I had a student ask if he could join my History Club. "Of course," I said. He thanked me up and down and told me that he needed to be out of his house as much as possible because his parents were never home and he was lonely. As time went on, he not only became an active member of the group, but later wound up on the homecoming court as a senior. I felt proud that our club had helped him gain the self-confidence to bloom.

Academic Activities

Many schools have nabbed the unsuspecting new teacher to help with strategies to improve academic achievement. Teachers may become involved in before or after-school tutoring, school-community partnerships, or other programs established by the school. Programs such as these are enormously satisfying to teachers who enjoy the opportunity to further assist students. These programs, often times promoted to meet accountability standards mandated by No Child Left Behind, are likely to have specific teacher and student accountability measures and expected outcomes. It is important to be aware of the expectations and work cooperatively with administrators to create a written document explaining the responsibilities, expected outcomes, and benefits.

A Word of Caution

Serving as a coach or advisor can be tremendously rewarding. However, as a novice teacher considerable thought must be given when deciding to add duties to an already very full plate. Remember that there will be many years in the future where you may be able to lend your expertise. If asked to serve as an advisor, it is quite respectable to say that while you would enjoy the opportunity, you would prefer to focus your attention on becoming the best teacher possible.

Your Life

That's right! You are actually allowed to have a life outside of the classroom. We commend teachers who arrive at school with the sunrise and leave by the light of the moon. Their commitment to excellence is well deserving of praise. At the same time, however, you must remember that activities outside the realm of teaching are not only needed, but also necessary. You must be able to separate from your job at the end of the school day.

The last section of the chapter will help you understand the "haves and have-nots" of your personal life outside of school. Some researchers estimate that upwards of 50% of all teachers leave the profession within five years due to stress factors such as unreal expectations, harsh working conditions, long hours, classroom discipline problems, and lack of administrative support.[11] In addition to the other hints offered in the book such as organization and planning, there are many ways to reduce the tension and stress of the job. Avoiding teacher burnout should be a priority from day one for all new teachers.

Burnout

Everyone knows someone who has lost it at work. Maybe they blew up and yelled, maybe they broke down and cried, or maybe they just walked out for good. Whatever the action, in each instance, it started long before the day they revolted. Teacher burnout is typically the result of extended periods of high stress and can lead to withdrawing, caring less, or even working to exhaustion.[12]

Burnout among teachers can come from a variety of sources, but three of the most common reasons are becoming too personally involved in the classroom, trying to be "Super-Teacher," and behavior management issues.

When students use obscenities and display other extreme misbehaviors in the classroom, it is important to step back and realize that the frustrated student may be not actually yelling at you - but rather at life. Students bring their anger into the classroom and often lash out at those closest to them; a.k.a. you. For instance, when a student tells a new teacher "where to go," the teacher reaction can be hurt, defensiveness, anger, or retaliation. All of these emotions, under certain circumstances, can push a teacher to the edge.

A novice teacher's temper can be pretty touchy at times. If a student crosses the line, a teacher may perceive it as a challenge to prove who is the boss. *A teacher never wins a power struggle with a student.* When kids lash out, try to see the situation from their perspective. Try to understand why this is happening, how you arrived there, and how you can help. Experienced teachers recognize that the problem rarely has to do with them personally, and try to find ways to help, with the assistance of the administration, if needed.

When you find yourself stressed out during the day, try to take a step back. Get a drink of water and breathe. It's truly amazing what a few moments of deep breathing can do for a person. It's equally amazing when you realize you haven't been breathing for hours! If you can, go outside and get fresh air. If that is not possible, go to a classroom window and open it. Nature is sometimes a great way to heal.

Lack of effective student discipline is the major cause of teacher stress and contributes strongly to why teachers choose to leave the profession. As will be emphasized in the chapter on classroom management, prior preparation, organization, and planning can help to eliminate these very common stressors.

Many educators start out rip-roaring and ready to be the "Super-teacher" with thoughts of jumping in there and changing the world with fresh teaching methods just learned in college. It is all right to change the world; but it is important to pace yourself while you are doing it. Not all methods will work the first time - and some may never work the way you planned. It's OK. It does not mean you are a bad educator. Too many teachers feel bad, for a lack of a better term, due to a few lessons not being up to snuff. Don't worry about that. Lessons are just that - lessons! They teach you what to do and how to fix problems.

Another characteristic of a young "Super-teacher" is the feeling that they must volunteer for every event that comes down the pike. If there is a need for a coach...they take it. If the school needs a chaperone for a dance...they do it. If the freshman class or local PTA group needs an adviser...they take it. If the building needs a new building representative...they volunteer. And on and on. Avoid putting too much on your plate. Leave time for yourself or you will drown in your own professionalism. The key is to know how much you can handle. If you feel yourself fading fast, eliminate some responsibility and take a break.

AN AUTHOR CASE STORY:

I have learned this lesson the hard way. When I began teaching, I took the job as athletic director of the junior high school where I was teaching. I had no real idea what I was doing, but I felt that a good employee helped anyway possible. I also was coaching softball at the high school. Everything worked out pretty well for the first year.

When I started teaching at the high school the following year, I began to load my plate. By year four I was Junior Varsity Baseball Coach, Ticket Manager (in charge of tickets, money disbursement, and profit reporting at ALL home sporting events), a union rep for my building, and advisor of the History Club. Oh yes! I also started thinking of a career in politics.

Lumped into all of this came the birth of my son, Kyle, which turned out to be the greatest blessing of my life. Kyle helped me to start thinking of myself again. It is not that I participated in all these activities out of obligation- not at all. I enjoyed each and every opportunity. However, Kyle's birth was a reminder that life outside of school activities has a place too. I worried that if I left my responsibilities I would not be as big a part of the school as before. I was dead wrong. Giving up coaching and some other outside responsibilities made me a better teacher and leader of the History Club, which I still advise.

The lesson here is to not spread yourself so thin that you can't do any of the jobs well. Some people thrive on always being busy. They may even say that you have a responsibility to the school to participate in activities. While that may be true to some extent, you must remember that the school would much rather have a happy and effective educator in the classroom, than a frustrated burnout that leaves the profession after three years. Beth Lewis[13] offers five tips to avoid teacher burnout:

1.   Ask for help when needed.

2.   Don't sweat the small stuff.

3.   Don't play the teacher at home.

4.   Take time for yourself, and

5.   Remember why you chose to teach.

Exercise

One of the best ways to avoid burnout is to get a regular dose of exercise. Whether it is running, racquetball, Pilates, volleyball, Tao Bo, cycling or walking, you need to incorporate at least 20 minutes of exercise per day into your normal weekly routine. We've all heard the reasons why people don't exercise. Top 10 reasons include "I don't have time, I can't stick to it, I never see any change, I can't afford a gym membership, and I hate it." To fit exercise into your day try the following: a) schedule your exercise time; b) keep a calendar to track you progress and stay motivated; and if you REALLY can't find 20 minutes a day, c) break it up into 10-15 minute segments by taking a brisk walk in the morning, taking a walk during your lunch, walking the stairs whenever possible, or walking the dog.[14]

AN AUTHOR CASE STORY:

Twelve years ago, while I was a student in college, I decided that I needed to find time for myself. The stress of college papers, deadlines, and overall work began to take a toll on my health - both physical and mental. Looking back on it now, the stress I was experiencing then would not even touch the level it would become as I entered the teaching profession - and started a family.

I began running three times a week. It started with a simple mile run/jog around the local track. As I got more and more into shape, I lengthened the distance slowly. By my first year of teaching I was running five miles five days a week. It has scaled off since then - I am now back down to three runs of three miles each week - but the overall effect on my life is obvious.

When I run, I am able to clear my mind. I use the time to listen to my favorite music and meditate. It is amazing how I am able to think so clearly and sort out problems that seemed insurmountable just a few hours earlier. When my run is finished, I have a sense of release and ease.

This is what exercise can do for you. A simple fifteen-minute walk around the block will allow you to free your mind. Take time to look at the trees or notice what kind of birds are flying overhead - hopefully not vultures! You will be amazed at how the problems of the world seem to fade a little bit. No problem ever goes away, but your frame of mind will determine how you handle the situation.

My wife has told me more that once to "Go run" when I have come home from work. She realizes my stress level and knows what exercise does. Likewise, when you feel stressed, you need to understand that your body is asking you for help. Finding a way to get rid of that negative energy will help you maintain your sanity - and your friends!

Exercise also allows many to sleep better at night. Some can hit the pillow and be out in two minutes, for others it might be two hours. It seems, for some, the mind kicks into high gear the minute they decide to rest. The days you exercise you may notice your mind is much less active when it's time to wind down and go to bed. Considering most experts claim you need at least eight hours of sleep per night, being able to get right to sleep will assure you are ready for the challenges the next day will bring.

A good rule of thumb is to make sure to give yourself four or five hours of post- exercise time before bed. If you exercise too close to bed time it may actually stimulate your brain and get you in a more active mode. So make sure you have time to wind down after physical activity.

You don't have to become a world-class athlete or win the Boston Marathon to benefit from exercise. The overall benefit to your mental and physical well being is immeasurable. Exercise generates energy and the more energy you have, the more productive you are likely to be each day.[5] Even as little as 20 minutes a day can work wonders for both mind and body. A little break from the stress of life goes a long way in helping you face problems from a new perspective. Many people take great pride in working 50 hours a week while expressing they have no time for themselves. While this may be what life is all about for some, you must realize that *you* come first. Take time out for yourself - not only because it will be good for you, but also because you deserve it!

"Quality Time" for yourself

While exercise will allow you time to think and talk to yourself, you also need to remember that you are entitled to enjoy the things that make you happy. Let's face it, one of the reasons people work is to be able to enjoy the "simple pleasures" life has to offer. While most educators truly enjoy teaching, many would still say that playing 18 holes of golf also sounds pretty good on most days.

Like exercising, you must give yourself time to enjoy life's rewards. Whether it's going to a movie once a week, reading a good book (not about your subject area), cooking a great meal, playing with your kids at the park, or just taking a simple nap, you must escape.

Now let's be careful not to paint a picture where each and every day you sprint out of the building screaming for it to all end. Teaching is a very rewarding experience - and those who enter the profession usually do so because they are committed to helping kids learn and grow. However, you still need to go home and enjoy that favorite hobby.

Sometimes a good time outside of work may include having a drink or meeting for a social hour at a local establishment. There are two schools of thought on this issue. Many a veteran teacher will say you have every right to go out for a drink every now and then. You are an adult and should be able to enjoy local establishments where alcohol is served. Likewise, you are also allowed to buy beer in the grocery store. Conversely, other teachers will drive to another town assuring they will not run into students or parents at the store with a Coors Light 30 pack in their cart. The bottom line is that you are an adult human being allowed to have a drink. However, as a teacher and technically an extended arm of the state, you bear a special burden to act as a responsible role model. Obviously, it would not paint a great community image if your car wore a path to the local watering hole. You are a role model for kids and public intoxication is a very embarrassing moment for any teacher. The parental and administrative response is never positive, and it may not bode well for future job security.

Some teacher contracts now include a "morality clause" to guard against such actions on the part of teachers. This clause could lead to the board taking action against a teacher for inappropriate behavior.

You must remember, like sports stars, part of the job of being an educator is living in a glass house. Everyone knows you, even if you don't know him or her. You are perceived as a leader in the community and an example of stability for the students. This responsibility is a part of your job as an educator. When you do go out, make sure that you keep in mind that *anyone* could be watching.

Try to think of what you would feel like to see one of your teachers stumbling intoxicated out of a bar. While you might have gotten a laugh out of it, your respect for that teacher went straight out the window. Don't let this happen to the career and image you work so hard to achieve. Go out and have fun on occasion, but be responsible.

Chapter Activities

Exercise #1: Mock Interview

The following exercise is the actual interview process used by an actual practicing administrator. Take a moment to review the "ground rules" and then practice the interview questions with a peer. It is also helpful to tape or video record the process so you can later painfully critique yourself. This exercise should be done as if it were the real thing. Your attire should be that of an actual interview. Take it seriously. After all, "practice makes perfect!"

The Interview Process – A Practicing Administrator's View

The interview process for a teaching position is a very important exercise. The first ten minutes are critical in determining the direction of the rest of the interview.

The candidate should be appropriately dressed for success. First impressions are important. I look for poise and confidence. A firm handshake during the introductions is important. It is also important for the candidate to look the interviewer in the eye. Eye contact is a sign of confidence; which is obviously an important component in the teaching profession.

Body language is equally vital. I want to see a candidate who is confident, attentive, and relaxed. Hands should be comfortably at the side or placed on the table. I certainly am not looking for someone who comes in with their arms crossed. This type of posture is closed and will come across to students in the classroom the same way.

When interviewing multiple candidates for a position, the interview team asks the same questions in order to compare responses. The team also asks questions which put the candidate in a position of having to generate on-the-spot responses.

Below are questions used by Larry Kisabeth in the interview process:

1. Tell us a little about yourself.

2. Why did you choose education?

3. Describe your teaching style.

4. What could I expect to see if I entered your classroom?

5. How do you motivate the student who has his head down at the back of the room?

6. If a fight breaks out in your room, what do you do?

7. Describe your behavior management system.

8. What is the importance of your textbook? How do you use it?

9. What is your experience with students on an Individual Education Plan? What does the IEP do for a student?

10. Respect for an educator is not often extended simply because of the title "teacher." How is *real* respect earned?

11. What makes you the best candidate for this position?

Consider This:

What are some other possible questions you may be asked in an interview? Come up with three more possible questions then openly share them with the rest of the class. Make a list of the questions and keep that list handy and refer back to it prior to entering your first real interview process. The more prepared you are walking in, the more likely you are to get a long, hard look from the employer, and hopefully...the job!

Exercise #2: Tell Us About Yourself

This is a question that is nearly guaranteed to rear its ugly head at every interview. This exercise is truly valuable and it is not as easy as it sounds! Practice with a peer by preparing what you want to express in two minutes or less. Responses that are too long, unrelated, or redundant can be a real turn-off to the interview team. Additional practice includes responding to, "tell me how your peers and/or cooperating teacher would describe you."

Exercise #3: Why Can't I Send This Resume and Cover Letter?

Review the following cover letter and resume and identify the errors. Rewrite the assignments so they could be presented to a school district.

Cover Letter

May 2007

Dr. Boyton
Futuristic School District
524 W. Madison
Roundtree, Mo

Dear Mr. Boynton,

I would like to apply for a teaching position at the elementary level. I heard that you will have openings this fall. I am sure there are many great things your district has to offer. Please consider me for these and any other elementary positions that may be available.

I am finishing up my methods block in second grade this week and will begin my student teaching experience in the fall in Kindergarten at Rountree in Springfield. This May, I will graduate from Southwest Missouri State University with a degree. I have always been commited to continuing my education. This summer I plan to begin work on a Master's in Reading degree. Later this month, I will attend a Wright Group integrated language arts workshop.

There are several reasons why your school is where I choose to be at. First of all, my emphasis is in early childhood education. In addition, I grew up not far from Roundtree, and since I plan to relocate to the community in which I teach, I would still be near to my family because we are very close. It also interests me that your school is hosting a Kagan Cooperative Learning workshop this summer. I have spent many hours working with a teacher who is trained in Kagan Cooperative Learning. I like the results I have seen, and have enjoyed experimenting with some of the structures myself.

I am a teacher because I enjoy hard working and helping others find success. I want my students to experience meaningful, interesting learning that applys to their lives. I believe this can be accomplished through the use of hands-on/minds-on activities, cooperative learning, an integrated curriculum, and, when possible, technology and the internet.

Please refer to the enclosed resume and list of references. I look forward to meeting with you to discuss your school's goals and how I can help you meet them as a teacher. I can be reached at (419/555-1213) until 3:00 p.m., or at home (419-352-0035) after 4 p.m., or at (419) 777-5467 on weekends at my boyfriends, or by cell at 419-350-2568. Thank you for your consideration.

In Anticipation

Bea A. Teacher

Enclosures

Resume

Ivana Job
iwantajob!@sbcglobal.net
215 University Drive
Collegeland, Ohio 12345
(555) 555-5555

Objective

To obtain a teaching job in a good district that values my skills.

Education

Bachelor of Science Degree in Education   Bowling green, Ohio. June 2006

- ❑   GPA 3.2
- ❑   Passed Praxis
- ❑   Worked 40 hours per week to finance coursework

Relevant Experience

Student Teaching Gaylord Elementary School   New York, NY. Jan 2006 –May 2006

- ❑   Managed class of 27 tenth grade graders
- ❑   Promoted postive school climate.
- ❑   Developed original literature units.
- ❑   Always offered to help in after school tutoring sessions for the OGT
- ❑   Served as an advisor to the Chess Club

Related Experience

Walmart, Customer Service Representative   Tiffin, Ohio Summers 2004-06

- ❑   Solved customer problems.
- ❑   Served as cashier
- ❑   Assisted customers with shopping

Help - A- Child Tutor   Bowling Green, OH. Fall, 2005

- ❑   Worked with 2 seventh graders on English Literature
- ❑   I created lesson plans that included homework assignments for them
- ❑   Maintained appropriate, accurate documentation

University Libraries Reference Assistant,Bowling Green, OH   Spring 2003-Spring 2006

- ❑   Assisted reference desk leader

Awards and Honors

- ❑   Bowling Green High School Honor Society.
- ❑   Kappa Phi Beta Academic Award Recipient

Special Skills

- ❑ Proficient in PhotoShop/Adobe Acrobat
- ❑ I have used both pc and Mac in college coursework.

References Upon Request

Chapter Summary

1. Seek out assistance from those who are familiar with the process.

2. Preparing for the interview by knowing the district, practicing common interview questions, and using positive non-verbal signs.

3. Develop competent submission materials.

4. Present a positive presence through your rapport building skills, professional dress, and time management skills.

5. Fully consider the positives and negatives of the district. Consider the culture of the community, the benefits package and the expectations of your position.

6. Practice the interview with a peer to become familiar with your presentation and gain confidence.

7. Consideration should be given to the time spent in the teacher's lounge to avoid negative burned-out teachers. Teachers should seek positive enthusiastic teachers who enjoy teaching.

8. New teachers who are interested in extracurricular activities should consider how the additional time will affect their instructional duties

Notes

1. Husser, W.J. (1999). *Predicting the need for newly hired teachers in the United States to 2008-09.* (National Center for Educational Statistics 1999-026). Retrieved from http://nces.ed.gov/programs quarterly/Vol1_1/1_4/3-esq14-g.asp.

2. Snyder, T. (2006, August). *Mini-Digest of Education Statistics in Education.* National Center for Educational Statistics. US Department of Education. Retrieved from http://nces.ed.gov/pubs2007/ 2007067.pdf.

3. Sadker, M. P. & Sadker, D. M. (2005). *Teachers, schools, and society. (7th ed.).* Boston, MA: McGraw Hill.

4. Peddle, M. T., Trott, C.E. & Bergeron, L. (2002). *Public teacher entry and retention in Illinois: Are there leaks in the pipeline?* Center for Governmental Studies Northern Illinois University. Retrieved from http://www.cgsniu.org/news/pdf/Public%20 Teacher%20Entry%20&%20 Retention%20in%20Illinois%20(July%202002).pdf.

5. The Interview. Career Search Guide available at www.bgsu.edu/ downloads/sa/file42419.pdf.

6. Purdue University Center for Career Opportunities. Retrieved from https:// www.cco.purdue.edu/Student/JobSearchSkills_Non Verbal.shtml?mode=p.

7. Raudsepp, E.(2002). *Bad body language can spoil an interview.* College Journal from the Wall Street Journal. Retrieved from www.collegejournal.com/ jobhunting/interviewing/20001114-raudsepp.html.

8. National comprehensive center for teacher quality and public agenda. (2007). *Lessons learned: New Teachers talk about their jobs, challenges and long range plans.* Retrieved from www.publicagenda.org.

9. United State Department of Labor, Bureau of Labor Statistics Occupational Outlook Handbook 2008-2009 Edition. Retrieved from www.bls.gov/oco/ ocos069.htm.

10. Ohio Revised Code Section 3319.08.

11. Surpuriya, T. & Jordan, M. (1997, October). Teacher burnout. Memphis Flyer. Retrieved from http://weeklywire.com/ww/10-27-97/memphis_cvr. html.

12. Farber, B. A. (1991). Crisis in education: Stress and burnout in the American teacher. San Francisco: Jossey-Bass.

13. Lewis, B. (2008) Avoiding teacher burnout. About.Com. Retrieved November 15, from http://k6educators.about.com/cs/helpforteachers/a/ avoidburnout.htm?p=1.

14. Waehner, P. (2007, July 19). The top 10 reason you don't exercise. About.Com. Retrieved from http://exercise.about.com/cs/fittingitin/a/ aexerciseobstacl.htm?p=1.

Appendix

Sample Resume

Ivana Job

iwantajob!@sbcglobal.net

Permanent Address
316 College Drive
Hometown, Ohio 0000
(555) 555-5555

Local Address
215 University Drive
Collegeland, Ohio 12345
(555) 123-4567

Objective

To assist with and advance the overall educational experience of high school students, especially in regard to their understanding of the history of the United States of America.

Education

- ❑ My State University   May 2005
- ❑ Masters Degree in Educational Administration
- ❑ My State, Ohio
- ❑ G.P.A. 4.00
- ❑ eacherland College
- ❑ Bachelor of Education Degree in History
- ❑ G.P.A. 3.64
- ❑ Ohio education certification grades 7-12

Related Experience

- ❑ Student Teaching Experience (if you have not held a teaching position)
  Teacher City, Ohio Spring Semester 2004
  - • List at least 2 duties beginning with a verb
  - • Created lesson plans from state standards
  - • Instructed five sections per day
- ❑ Education City Schools- US History Teacher
  Bay Watch, Falls, MI Fall 2004 - Present
  - • Aligned curriculum to state standards
  - • Maintained 97% passage rate on state assessments
  - • Served as Social Studies Department Chairperson
- ❑ Summer Intervention Education Program and Summer School
  Bay Watch Falls, MI. Summer 2004 and 203
  - • Provided intervention activities for students aged 14 - 17
  - • Implemented and managed program curriculum

Ivana Job, page 2

- ❏ Help – A – Child Tutor
  Main Street Elementary School, Fall 2003

  - • Planned and implemented assessments for sophomore history students
  - • Collaborated with two classroom teachers on Individual Education Plans

Relevant Experience

- ❏ Junior Varsity Baseball Coach
  Top Score, MI. 1997-1998

  - • Mentored and coached team of 17 young men
  - • Advanced team to finals two consecutive years
- ❏ Assistant Varsity Softball Coach
  Top Score, MI. 1994-1996

  - • Assisted head coach with all aspects of team management
  - • Worked with team on monthly fundraising activities

Professional Accomplishments

- ❏ Education High School Teacher of the Year (2003)
- ❏ Nominated for County Teacher of the Year (2003)
- ❏ Heidelberg College Cooperating Teacher of the Year (2003)
- ❏ Nominated for State of Ohio Cooperating Teacher of the Year (2003)

Honors

- ❏ Awarded EIF Williams Student Teaching Award Heidelberg College (1994)
- ❏ Member of Who's *Who Among America's Teachers* (2001, 2002, 2005, 2006, 2007)

Campus Activities

- ❏ American Council of Social Studies Teachers-Student Chapter
- ❏ Sigma Gamma Thai Fraternity
- ❏ Dance Marathon Site Coordinator

Additional Skills

- ❏ Proficient on X-Box System 3
- ❏ Proficient in Mandarin Chinese

References Available Upon Request

Sample Cover Letter

316 College Drive
Hometown, Ohio 0000
March 19, 2008

Dr. Robert T. Goodsun, Director of Curriculum
Gotena City Schools
567 Main Street
Besttown, OH 44444

Dear Dr. Goodsun:

Having completed my student teaching experience in the elementary cognitive disabilities unit at Bowling Green Elementary School in Bowling Green, Ohio, I look forward to beginning my teaching career. As a graduate of Gotena City Schools I am familiar with your outstanding academic history and it would be an honor to be a part of such excellence. In May, I will graduate from Bowling Green State University with licensure in elementary cognitive disabilities. Mrs. Nicely, the second grade teacher at Greatness Elementary School, notified me of a possible opening in the elementary unit for the upcoming year. As highlighted in the enclose resume, my academic achievements, related teaching experience, and volunteer activities demonstrate that I am prepared to embark on a rewarding teaching career.

Educating students with special needs necessitates the ability to communicate effectively with all stakeholders in the school community, including parents, teachers, administrators, care providers, and community agencies. I believe my practicum evaluations speak to my abilities in that area. My additional coursework afforded the opportunity to engage in practicum experiences with students in high and low incidence classrooms, in both inclusive and self-contained classrooms. Additionally, I have written and implemented Individualized Education Plans, participated in Multi-factored Evaluations, and worked daily with other special service providers.

As a student at Bowling Green State University, I have held leadership positions in the Delta Sorority Student Government Association and served for a one-year term as treasurer for the student chapter of Exceptional Children. As an honor student I am dedicated, organized, hardworking, compassionate and strive for high academic standards. Bowling Green has provided a well-rounded experience and I believe I have taken advantage of all available opportunities to grow as an educator.

I look forward to the opportunity to discuss my qualifications for the position of teacher of elementary cognitive disabilities for the Gotena City Schools. I will contact you within two weeks discuss the possibility of a meeting. I can be reached at (555) 555-5555. Thank you for taking the time to review my materials and considering me for your teaching staff.

Sincerely

Ivana Job

Enclosures

Sample Philosophy of Education

John Dewey once said, "To find out what one is fitted to do, and to secure an opportunity to do it, is the key to happiness." I am on the path to happiness because I believe teaching is what I am fitted to do and my education should secure my opportunity to do so. As a teacher I know that each and every day I will have the opportunity to make a difference in the lives of students. The importance of my role as a future educator cannot be understated because of the impact I will have on society through the growth of my students. In the following paragraphs you will read about my philosophical orientation, my theory of behavior management, and the educational learning theory that I plan to use in my classroom.

After analyzing my personality type and style of teaching, I consider myself to be an idealist. I view teachers as leaders for their students. I also feel that teachers should always model positive behaviors, values, and ideals. Idealists conduct their classroom in an authoritarian, teacher centered environment while facilitating analytical thought processes. The role of the student in an idealist's classroom is to absorb and expand on the ideals shared by their teacher.

Managing the classroom is a critical key to teaching success. My classroom will model B.F. Skinners theory of behavior modification. The Skinnerian model appears to be closely aligned with my views on behavior management as he believed that children are born as "blank slates," cannot be self governing and need to be "shaped" by adults to produce appropriate behaviors. Idealists believe in high teacher control through the use of this authoritarian style of discipline.

Through careful examination of different educational learning theories in my classes and through field experience, I have come to the conclusion that I am a supporter of Howard Gardner's theory of multiple intelligences. Gardner's theory proposes that there are eight independent ways in which the human brain processes information. In order to apply Gardner's theory to classroom practices, lessons must be designed to appeal to a number of these intelligences. Among others, some of these ways include verbal, intrapersonal, logical, and spatial. In doing this, information will be transmitted to students in multiple ways, and through this process, students can learn using the most effective method.

Since my duty as a future educator is to provide my students with the best education possible, I have put time and thought into developing my personal educational philosophy. As a future teacher, I realize how privileged I am to have the opportunity to make a difference in the lives of many children. I see today's children as the future of our country and as a teacher I am therefore responsible for educating the nation's prospective leaders, business persons, and industrial workers. I desire to improve as a future educator so that I can help prepare students to be successful, contributing members of society.

2

THE LIFE AND TIMES OF A TRUE PROFESSIONAL

After the researching, applying, interviewing, resume writing, and the job offers-- finally came that anticipated day when I arrived in my classroom for the very first time. It was surreal, exhilarating, and scary, all at the same time. Exhilarating because I was finally fulfilling my plan; scary because I now had my marching orders with no buffer between me and the real world. Through the rose colored glasses of a novice, I did not even notice the cold cement walls and the insurmountable tome of items left piled high from corner to corner. Fortunately I had four weeks before school started to take a skeleton of a classroom and make it into a functioning, learning-friendly place for second graders.

I arrived at my school that first time with my parent's van filled to capacity with all of the teaching materials and equipment I had accumulated for many years. I can remember wanting to be a teacher from my early days of elementary school. Since that time, I had saved countless workbooks, storybooks, games, posters, craft kits, office supplies, and a plethora of other items for use in my classroom. After toting all my boxes upstairs to my classroom, the true weight of the task before me settled in as I finally seemed to grasp the overwhelming picture of my stacks of boxes along with the boxes left in the room.

The second grade teacher who occupied the room for nearly 20 years before opting to move up to sixth grade had fortunately left behind many games, books, and other teaching supplies. In addition to the boxes of items sitting in the center of the room, I had four large closets and three large shelving units packed full of resources to be reviewed, inventoried and organized.

For a week in 90 degree plus degree heat, I took absolutely everything out of every box, every closet, and off of every shelf and practically asked myself, "Do I ever see myself using this?" Anytime the answer was no, it went in the trash. For example, there were nearly 50 old children's library books marked "discard" dating back to the 1950s and earlier. These books had seen a lot of love but were very outdated. My Scholastic Book Club collection would easily replace those. After everything had been read, sorted, categorized, and organized, I began the process of putting everything away in the closets and on the shelves. Even now, three years later, I am still moving things around and reorganizing the room.

After I had everything put away, I had to begin setting up the furniture in the room. I knew I would be having 23 students (I later learned never to plan on an exact number of students until at least the third day of school, and even then the number can still change). I arranged the desks in a U shape—a workable formation used by my cooperating teacher when I was student teaching. Once the students' desks were arranged, the rest of the room, including my desk, the computers, and the table for reading groups all fell into place.

Now I was finally ready to begin getting the classroom ready for that first day. I spent hours laminating the many posters, banners, and signs to help brighten up the otherwise drab cement block walls of the classroom. I hung up 12 birthday cakes with student birthdays, put up cardinal direction signs, replaced the 1950's Zaner-Bloser alphabet cards, added a monthly calendar, daily weather chart, and counting straws, constructed an "All About Mr. Turner" board, a "Welcome To Second Grade" collage and "Our Goals For The Year" which featured letters the students wrote at the end of their first grade year about what they would like to learn in second grade.

I also started planning classroom management techniques. I created a lunch count signup method by writing BUYING and PACKING on two sentence strips and attached them to the chalk sill. I wrote each student's name with a fine-tipped marker on a close pin and clipped them all to the PACKING side of the strip. Students take care of signing up for lunch by moving their clothespin to buying if they plan to purchase a lunch or leave it on packing if they brought a lunch. One of the classroom jobs is "lunch count": a student counts the number of clothes pins on the buying side, fills out the lunch count slip and delivers it to the cafeteria. Other classroom jobs I created before the first day of school included paper passer, line leader (boy and girl), officer messenger, scrap patrol, chair patrol, and calendar manager. These jobs are rotated every two weeks, allowing students to become "experts" at their jobs before training the next student assigned. I also purchased a "flip card" chart to help students monitor their own behavior in class. Students who misbehave have to "flip a card" starting with green and moving through four other colors before arriving at a red card. Each step along the way comes with a consequence.

The very last part of preparing the classroom actually involved planning lessons for the first week. I had to go through all of the textbooks and decide which ones I would be putting on the students' desks and which ones I would be saving for later in the year. I went through a large filing cabinet of papers that had been left with the room, along with many workbooks, teacher's manuals, and other resources of my own before finally starting to make some notes in the lesson planning book. When the students arrived on that first day, the countless hours of preparatory work in the classroom beforehand had finally paid off.

So you can see that early planning where possible is essential to getting prepared for those smiling faces. If at all possible, allow one full month of classroom preparation *before that first day because preparing can make all the difference in the world as to how successful or unsuccessful that first day and that first year turns out to be.*

Aaron Turner is a 2nd grade teacher at Johnsville Elementary School in Northmor Local, Ohio

Aaron's story vividly highlights the range of emotions, activities, and stages new teachers may experience as they embark on preparing for their very first classroom, in their very first year of their very first school. You too may experience much of the same. Every summer in late August, teachers lie awake wondering what the new school year will bring. One might think of the new students who will enter their room. Or, one may wonder about how the year will unfold. And, of course, they get nervous. That's right! Nervous! A veteran teacher once said, "The day you don't get nervous on the first day of classes, start looking for another line of work." Of course novice and veteran teachers likely get nervous for different reasons. Novice teachers for what they *do not* know........and veteran teachers for what they *do* know! So how will you move from novice to vet? Researcher Lilian Katz [1] contends that no one, not lawyers, engineers, nor podiatrists, can begin their profession as a veteran, and the teaching profession is no exception. Katz believes that professional growth occurs sequentially in both thought and behavior as the novice learns to adapt to the position requirements. Ellen Moir, [2] a California educator, asserts that typically all first year teachers travel through five stages:

(a) anticipation, (b) survival, (c) disillusionment, (d) rejuvenation and (e) reflection.

The anticipation phase is when you are filled with the excitement of gaining your first new teaching position. You cannot wait to get your classroom and your students and begin your exciting career. The survival stage is characterized by feeling overwhelmed by everything that is unfamiliar and new. There is much to learn in a short period of time, and there may be stressful issues that arise. Moir notes that "despite teacher preparation programs, new teachers are caught off guard by the realities of teaching." [2] While trying to deal with the day-to-day responsibilities, you are fighting to stay on top of everything. You are working at school and taking work home and often feel like you are just surviving. It is during the survival stage where new teachers are likely to become ill and feel very, very tired. After a couple of months in survival mode, disillusionment sets in. This may be when you sit back and say, *Why did I become a teacher?* Additionally, you may be feeling that no one told you about the planned meetings, impromptu meetings, parent nights, conferences, collaboration with special teachers (speech therapist, reading specialist, occupational therapist, and behavior specialist), documenting student behavior, differentiating classroom instruction, and managing student behavior. This is a most challenging time because the stress can be a strong influence on relationships with family and friends. The stress may also disrupt proper eating, necessary sleeping, exercise patterns, and engaging in hobbies. Once a novice teacher finds their way through the disillusionment stage, a renewed sense of confidence begins to build. The rejuvenation phase typically occurs following the winter break. The time away from the school environment may afford the new teacher a chance to

- ❏ "reconnect" with family and friends,

- ❏ relax,

- ❏ return to normal eating habits,

- ❏ exercise,

- ❏ reestablish sleeping habits,

- ❏ participate in recreational activities and hobbies,

- ❏ reflect, and

- ❏ have fun.

During the time away from school, you begin to reflect on the first half-year. You begin to think of a hundred strategies to improve the experience. When you return to school, feeling rested and rejuvenated, you walk the halls a step farther from a novice and closer to a vet. The last stage is the reflection stage, which begins as the year is winding down. The light is clear and bright at the end of the tunnel, and with a year of experiences under your belt, you have a great story to tell! Before the year is over you are already planning great things for the next year. Remembered are the great experiences and minimized are the not so great ones. Moir [2] offers that the first year teacher gains:

- ❏ coping skills,

- ❏ long term planning skills,

- ❏ a better understanding of the school environment,

- ❏ a more complete understanding of curriculum matters,

- ❏ a sense of accomplishment,

- ❏ professional pride,

- ❏ an increased status as a "not so new" teacher; and

- ❏ new instructional strategies.

Teaching is exciting and rewarding and it is also dynamic and variable each and every year. So regardless of what stage you are currently operating, nerves can be a signal of excitement. They may signify that you want to do your job well. You want students to succeed and learn in a way that will impact lives forever. That awesome responsibility demands a tiny bit of nervous reaction. So when you feel the jitters when that first period bell rings. Good for you! This chapter will cover your role as a professional in your school district.

The True Professional

Professionalism is a part of every school day, whether you are interacting with students, parents, colleagues, or community members. Society has high expectations for its teachers; often higher than other professions. Teachers play a major role in promoting democratic principles and creating educated citizens, as hard as that may be some days! We share a huge responsibility for shaping the minds of children, and a few parents too. Effective teachers are committed to the social, emotional, and academic growth of students. And most importantly researchers say that teachers influence student achievement more than *any* other factor in the classroom. [3] James Stronge notes that, "Teachers have a powerful, long-lasting influence on students. They directly affect how students learn, what they learn, how much they learn, and the ways they interact with one another and the world around them." [4] As a teacher you impact students' lives in many, many ways. Everyone can recall a favorite teacher who positively affected his or her life. So what makes an effective teacher? The answers to this question may vary to some degree. Some descriptions of effective teaching may include being knowledgeable, dedicated, caring, creative, service-oriented, as well as a reflective practitioner. Reflective teachers continually evaluate what they do in an attempt to meet the changing needs of the students. Teaching is unique because it deals with "humanware" not "hardware."

Despite what we know from research, you may hear someone say that anyone can teach. As a trained professional with specialized knowledge, you should know that everyone CANNOT do what you do. Consider the following "sample" lesson:

Divide your class of 30 students into six groups of five.

1. Instruct them to discuss in groups the negative effects of the Cold War, drawing on the fundamental basis of their own conclusions gathered from the factual class discussions during the past several days.

2. Have the students then write a three-page response on what they have learned from each other, properly citing their references. Collect at the end of class. Review and administer the end of the unit exam.

Yes, the above example may be a bit extreme, but the notion that every student is an open book with his/her mind ready and waiting to anxiously soak up all available knowledge molecules, is not always true. Effective teaching is a skillful blend of abilities gained from both practical and educational experiences. This is where *YOUR* "pedagogy" or art of teaching is crucial. The "teacher" engaged in the "lesson" above may possess the content knowledge about the Cold War, but is clearly not trained in pedagogy. You know that the lesson above would not be practical for any number of reasons. How do you know that? Because your professional training has taught you that content knowledge is only as useful as the teacher's ability to make the content *meaningful for the student.*

Is teaching a profession? Before becoming a principal in 2011, former fifth grade teacher Dr. Chad Warnimont of Perrysburg, Ohio, offered his perspective on professionalism below.

A few days before the beginning of the school year, I looked around the classroom with a sense of excitement. Without realizing it, creating a student-friendly learning environment was one of the first ways I demonstrated professionalism as a teacher. The physical classroom environment was inviting and welcoming, with math, science, and reading posters hanging around the room. Additionally, the classroom environment was positive, happy, and focused on learning. The atmosphere within my classroom illustrated dedication, commitment, and excitement for learning, displaying professionalism to any welcome visitor.

During the first few weeks of the school year, I was focused on conveying my professionalism to students, parents, and staff members. Professionalism in the classroom starts with being fair and equitable with all students. From the very first day, the students in my classroom knew my expectations for them. The first week of school, together as a class, we created learning expectations. We then held each other accountable for appropriate behavior.

Establishing a positive home/school connection is another form of professionalism that is necessary for a successful school year. When meeting parents on Preview Night, I created a preview packet with useful information about fifth grade. This was the first step in developing a meaningful rapport with parents. Throughout the year, this connection with home strengthened, and I gained credibility through on-going communication with parents that highlighted student successes and identified areas for improvement.

The last aspect of professionalism is working collaboratively with colleagues. Being the new teacher on the team, I used this opportunity to listen and observe successful teaching practices. Additionally, as a participating member of the team, I voiced opinions and provided feedback to my colleagues when making decisions.

Professionalism is built upon throughout the year when working positively with students, parents, and staff members. Valuing students and parents as individuals creates a culture of respect and professionalism. Listening, observing, and collaborating with colleagues contributes to a professional working culture focused on meeting students' needs. That first school year helped me gain confidence in my abilities, which encouraged and strengthened my communication skills with interested stakeholders.

Using Powell's [5] ten-item definition of a *full professional* below, can you identify some actions, thoughts, or belief's from Chad's story that reflect professionalism?

❑   Provides an essential service no other group can provide,

❑   Requires unique knowledge and skills acquired through extensive initial and on-going study/training,

❑   Involves intellectual work in the performance of duties,

❑   Commits to service and competence,

❑   Identifies *performance standards* that guide practice,

❑   Allows for a considerable amount of autonomy and decision-making,

❑   Accepts individual responsibility for decisions and actions,

❑   Enjoys prestige and public trust:

❑   Self governance (association) admits, polices, and excludes members; and

❑   Granted higher-than-average financial rewards.

Chad's case story definitely illustrates behaviors indicative of professionalism. And more importantly *Chad knows* he is a professional. He would probably wonder why we are even asking such a question.

While it is evident that teaching *is* a profession, teachers have been traditionally under-compensated as compared to other professionals such as those in the medical and legal fields. Why is this so? First, teaching, like social work, is considered a helping profession. Helping professions develop people. Nurturing the development of another human being is not an exact science with a formula of what to do when. Nor are teachers compensated for the amount of human potential they develop in any given day. Everyone receives the same great benefit for the same price. Because teaching is variable, an effective teacher must possess the unique knowledge, skills, intelligence, and innovation to diagnose and meet student needs. Secondly, since colonial times, the profession of teaching has been a field largely occupied by women, and professions dominated by women have been historically undercompensated and undervalued.

In the last decade, there have been steady increases in teacher pay, and the majority of teachers report they are satisfied with their chosen profession and would not change their career choice. [6] In recent decades, organizations have been increasingly dedicated to raising the standards of teaching and promoting professionalism. The National Council for Accreditation of Teacher Education (NCATE) is an agency that works with colleges promoting professionalism by establishing accreditation standards for teacher preparation programs. Accreditation through NCATE is voluntary and 525 of the nation's 1200 teacher preparation programs are accredited. Forty-six states currently utilize NCATE standards to evaluate teacher preparation programs.[7] Another organization dedicated to teacher professionalism is the National Board for Professional Teaching Standards.

National Board for Professional Teaching Standards

The release of *A Nation at Risk* (discussed later in chapter 5) drew critical attention to the quality of education, and two other critical publications in the 1980's focused attention on the training of the nation's teachers. *Tomorrow's Teachers* [7] and *A Nation Prepared,* [8] written by the Holmes Group and the Carnegie Forum respectively, advocated increased professionalism through increased standards and stricter educational requirements. Despite rigorous demands, teachers do not often receive the same respect afforded other careers.

A profession may also be defined as a specialized occupation or vocation, characterized by intensive training, involving the application of specialized knowledge of a subject, field or science and licensed by a governing body. [9] The National Board for Professional Teaching Standards (NBPTS) was created in 1987 following a meeting of the Carnegie Forum on Education. The goal of NBPTS is to recognize and reward extra ordinary teachers whose skills and knowledge indicate a high level of achievement.[10] The vision of NBPTS is simply to prepare teachers for what they *should know and be able to do*. The five core propositions include: [11]

1. Teachers are committed to students and their learning.

2. Teachers know the subjects they teach and how to teach those subjects.

3. Teachers are responsible for managing and monitoring student learning.

4. Teachers think systematically about their practice and learn from experience.

5. Teachers are members of learning communities.

A teacher wishing to achieve National Board Certification must go through a yearlong process of self-evaluation. This process is very strenuous, but rewarding. It involves writing, taping, and reacting to your own style of teaching. For some, self-reflection is a challenging process. However, it can prove to be very rewarding. Nearly 64,000 teachers in the United States have become National Board Certified teachers.[12] Some states reward teachers who achieve this prestigious milestone. For more information on becoming a National Board Certified educator, you can visit the website at www.nbpts. org.

The Ethics of Teaching

"Law tells us what we can and can't do, and ethics tell us what we should and shouldn't do." [13] Perhaps the most essential characteristic of professionalism is behaving in a manner beyond reproach. "Ethics is a collection of moral standards by which each person should be guided in their private and professional life. It tells us right from wrong, and how to live moral lives. The teaching profession evaluates the totality of behavior of an individual and its potential influence on others, in this case, students." [13] The ability to make ethical decisions involves effectively contemplating, analyzing, synthesizing, and diagnosing situations to make the most advantageous decision for all involved. Ethical decision-making is one of the most important behaviors in which teachers must engage daily on some level. Howe[14] describes six desirable characteristics for teachers when making ethical judgments:

1. Appreciation: for moral deliberation: ability to see complex moral dimensions of a problem and realize that care is needed to protect all rights of parties;

2. Empathy: ability to "walk in someone else's shoes;"

3. Knowledge: facts that enable us to put issues into context;

4. Reasoning: reflecting systematically on an issue and moving step-by-step to a conclusion;

5. Courage: the will power to act in what we perceive to be right, rather than just the familiar; and

6. Interpersonal skills: communicating about issues sensitively and tactfully.

There is no substitute for the specialized professional and pedagogical knowledge gained in teacher preparation programs. Field experiences and student teaching are necessary avenues to afford preservice teachers time to explore teaching in a real classroom. If a college has done its homework by choosing engaged cooperating teachers, student teaching can be a productive experience, preparing the novice for life on the "outside." In fact, many colleges have started exposing students to the real classroom beginning in their freshman year. This has assisted in "weeding out" students not suited for teaching, while at the same time shaking others loose of the classroom jitters.

As you have likely gathered or will soon learn, teachers are expected to be many things to many people. In addition to the *hard skills* associated with content knowledge, teachers are expected to have the *soft skills* associated with professionalism and ethics.[15] Hard skills refer to the technical components of a job or task, such as your lesson planning, instructional strategies, assessment procedures, and knowledge of content standards. Hard skills are generally easy to see, easy to measure, and easy to evaluate for quality. Soft skills on the other hand are often called "people skills." People skills refer to the ability to relate to people, deal with unexpected "people" dilemmas, and deal with everyday conflict. Teachers deal with all of these situations nearly each and every day and *people skills are essential* to be successful. As a teacher, strong professionalism and ethics are required for both hard and soft skills. Educators are expected to demonstrate professionalism and ethical behavior both in and out of the classroom. College and teacher preparation programs can teach and assess the acquisition of hard skills. Soft skills are more difficult to teach, hard to measure and nearly impossible evaluate.

Know Your School Personnel and School Support Systems

An important aspect of professionalism is cultivating positive relationships with colleagues in the building and the school district. Most school districts, whether large or small have a similar organizational structure. Most school districts are organized in a hierarchical structure with the school board at the top of the pyramid and the students at the lowest level. The school board is essentially the guiding entity for the district and is responsible for hiring two individuals; the superintendent and the treasurer. The duties of the school board and the superintendent are discussed in more detail in chapter five. In the district organization, the superintendent, treasurer, and assistant superintendents are typically housed in the "district central office" or "administrative building." Depending on the size of the district or the number of students, there may be from one to six assistant superintendents. In a very large district there may also be directors under each assistant superintendent. Each assistant superintendent will be responsible for a specific discipline of the district. As the School District Flow Chart on page 43 indicates, instructional personnel, such as teachers fall under the assistant superintendent for curriculum and instruction. In your building there will be a principal and maybe an assistant principal. Some buildings also have department heads and team leaders. Teachers will report to one of them depending on the building structure.

Day to day decisions are handled at the building level and it is important to find your "direct report" so that you will know to whom you should take concerns, issues, or questions. Maintenance of the proper *chain of command* in a "line" relationship is very important and "jumping" an administrative line of authority is not taken lightly. A line relationship depicts a distinct position hierarchy. Concerns are communicated first to your direct report for resolution. If for some reason a situation is not resolved, the next individual to contact should be your building principal. If indeed a teacher feels the need to contact personnel at the district central office, it should be *only after* the matter or concern has been thoroughly discussed with the building principal.

The building principal is a very important position and often sets the tone or climate of the building. Administration, writes Morrison,[16] involves the management of the schools' business and involves putting into everyday practice the policies established by the state legislature, state board of education, and the local board of education. Your administrative team is responsible for a myriad of duties to ensure you have tools to be the most effective teacher possible. Duties in which your administrative team may be involved include, but are not limited to:

- ❑ Maintaining the facilities for safety,

- ❑ Interviewing new personnel,

- ❑ Evaluating teachers and staff,

- ❑ Securing substitute teachers,

- ❑ Scheduling,

- ❑ Monitoring students (lunchroom, halls),

- ❑ Maintaining teacher supplies,

- ❑ Monitoring school budgets— approving teacher sick and vacation leave,

Typical School District Flow Chart

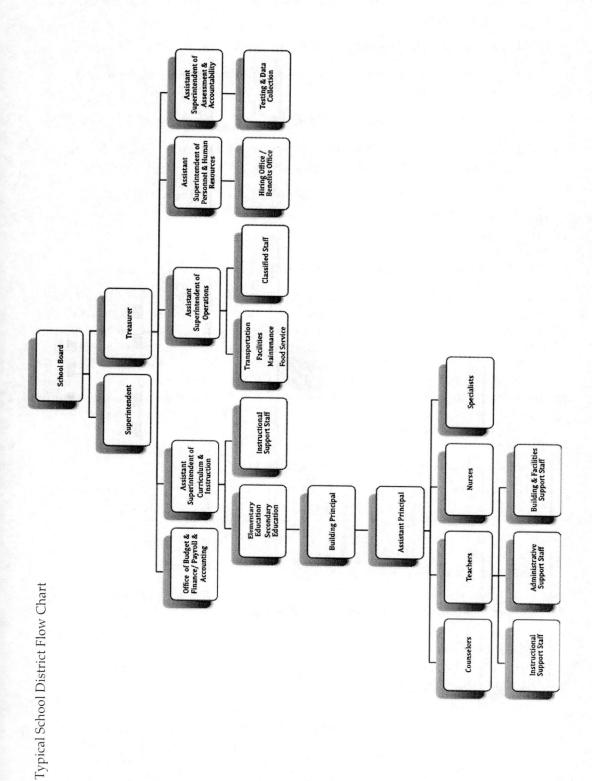

❑ Creating and maintaining correspondence (phone calls, letters, e-mail, newsletters),

❑ Assigning classrooms and developing student rosters,

❑ Writing reports dealing with accountability at the local, state and federal level,

❑ Interpreting and disseminating data,

❑ Instructing leadership (monitoring curriculum, providing relevant research and information to teachers),

❑ Coordinating classified staff (secretarial, cafeteria, maintenance, transportation),

❑ Writing grants; and

❑ Maintaining relationships with school and community groups.

In addition to the building administrators, there will be any number of staff in your building. Instructional staff and instructional support staff include all licensed and credentialed personnel responsible for student instruction. These individuals are considered to be in a "staff" relationship; meaning all are on the same hierarchical level, with none being considered "higher" than the other. Administrative support staff and school support staff, while not considered to be on the same authority level as instructional staff, are often the individuals who ensure the building runs smoothly. Can you think of ways that administrative and support staff promote success in school?

Instructional Staff and Instructional Support Staff:

Teachers, Reading Specialists, Title I Teachers, Behavior Interventionalists, Special Education Teachers, Department Head, Team Leader, Library/Media Specialist, Counselors, Nurses, Social Service Personnel, Psychologists, Occupational Therapists, Physical Therapists, Speech Therapists

Administrative Support/ Classified Staff:

Secretary, Transportation Personnel (bus, van drivers), Maintenance Personnel, Building & Grounds Personnel, Security Personnel

School Support Staff:

Paraprofessionals (regular and special needs), Tutors, Cafeteria Aides, Playground Aides, Bus Aides

The individuals who make up the office and the administrative staff of the school can be tremendous allies as you embark on your first teaching position. While some will greet you at the door, provide a personal tour and a welcome lunch, others may appear preoccupied, overworked and aloof. You may even serve under several different principals in your career. Each will have his/her own style. Some will be like Joe Clark in the 1998 movie "Lean on Me"; others will be more like Plato or Socrates, and still others will be like Houdini's best disappearing act. Regardless of the leadership style, it is an invaluable opportunity for you to develop collegial relationships. That is not to say that you will not have to compromise now and then. The point here is a vital one—an open line of communication must be established between your classroom and the office.

Students as Customers

You may notice that the most important people in the school have not been mentioned….that's right the students! Unfortunately, if represented on the organizational chart, they would be at the very bottom. This seems strange since the students are the reason we do what we do. Most like to think of the students as our *customers*. As educators, our goal is to provide each of our customers the best service possible. The best service is not always the easiest path and it takes a team effort. The saying, "It Takes a Village to Raise a Child," was popularized in the mid nineties by then first lady Hillary Clinton, and has much symbolism here. Said to be an African proverb, the saying speaks to the need for educators to be aware of and use all available support staff to meet the needs of each child. Working with a team at any level at any job takes three things: COMMUNICATION, COMMUNICATION, COMMUNICATION. Effective communication is created through active relationship building with the use of your soft skills.

Regardless of the school situation, it is important that you make adequate attempts to cultivate positive relationships with your administrative team. They are people who, just like you, have jobs to do: really big jobs. The beginning and closing of school can be particularly busy for the administrators and staff in your building. So…if they do not seek you out---FIND THEM! You are most likely on their "to do list," and they will appreciate your effort. The relationship you build with your building administrators should be on a one-on-one level, and it should begin before the first day of school.

In addition to your administrators and support staff, it is essential that you cultivate positive relationships as soon as possible with perhaps two of the most important individuals in your school: the secretary and the custodian. It will not be a difficult task if you keep in mind the following two thoughts: (a) *Treat others the way you wish to be treated, and* (b) *Your job teaching is no more important than any other individual's in the school.* Consider who will be fixing your lights, alerting you to messages from home, putting up hooks in your room, assisting you with the jammed copier, keeping a list of needed supplies, vacuuming your room, and greeting parents with whom you will meet. This means treating *all* employees working in the school with respect. Speak to all staff members in the morning when you see them in the hallway, and address them with the same deference as do teachers. Helpful hint: lose the word custodian—use "building operator" or "building engineer." Additionally, always refer to the secretary by name. Believe us, such titles will assist in moving your requests to the top of the "to do" list!

Preparing for your first *successful* year is a thoughtful and purposeful process and among the most pivotal events in your teaching career. Preparation is the most important key to creating a positive learning climate for you and your students. In the words of Pearl S. Buck: *"Only the brave should teach. Only those who love the young should teach. Teaching is a vocation. It is as sacred as the priesthood, as innate a desire, as inescapable as the genius, which compels a great artist. If he has not the concern for humanity, the love of living creatures, the vision of the priest and the artist, he must not teach."* [17]

Class Exercises

1. Choose a school district and examine their web site. What information is provided that will be helpful in organizing a positive learning climate? What is the key information that you will need to seek outside of the web site? Who would you contact?

2. In groups, investigate websites on a variety of subjects and distribute the information to the rest of the class. Possible topics: Classroom Management, Lesson Planning, Teaching in Multiple Rooms, Planning with Multiple Preps, Student/Teacher Desk Placement Options, Storing Materials, Parent Communication Options, Bulletin Board Ideas, Lighting for Success, Classroom Music, and Cheap Material Shopping Sites for New Teachers.

3. Use a search engine to research the *Teach for America Program*. Discuss the program's implications on teacher professionalism.

4. Make a list of 3 – 5 ethical dilemmas in which a teacher may have to deal. How do you believe they should be handled?

5. Choose a school district, search their web site and find out what teacher's union is available to join? What do they offer for teachers? How can their services assist your teaching career?

Chapter Summary

1. Most new teachers experience five phases during their first year: anticipation, survival, disillusionment, rejuvenation, and reflection.

2. Teachers influence student achievement more than any other factor.

3. A profession is a specialized occupation or vocation characterized by intensive training, involving the application of specialize knowledge of a subject, field, or science and licensed by a governing body.

4. The National Council for Accreditation of Teacher Education works with colleges promoting professionalism through voluntary teacher education standards.

5. The National Board for Professional Teaching Standards was created to recognize and reward extraordinary teachers. Becoming a National Board Certified Teacher is a high achievement and a sign of exceptional professionalism.

6. Professionalism is essential for effective teaching and ethical decision-making is one of the most important behaviors in which a teacher must engage.

7. Effective teachers need to possess both hard and soft skills.

8. As a novice teacher it is essential that collegial relationships are formed with key school personnel.

9. Schools have instructional staff, support staff, administrative support staff and administrators that operate in line and staff structures.

Notes

1. Katz, L. G. The Developmental Stages of Teachers - Retrieved from http://ceep.crc.uiuc.edu/pubs/katz-dev-stages.html. First published in 1972 under the title "The Developmental Stages of Preschool Teachers" in *Elementary School Journal* [73(1), 50-54].

2. As cited by the Wisconsin Education Association. (2011). Phases of First-Year Teaching. Retrieved from http://www.weac.org/professional_resources/new_teacher_resources/beg_handbook/phases.aspx Periods.

3. Darling-Hammond, L. (1999). *Teacher quality and student achievement: A review of state policy evidence.* Seattle, WA : Center for the Study of Teaching and Policy, University of Washington; Rivkin, S.G., Hanushek, E.A..,& Kain, J. F.(1998). *Teachers, schools and academic achievement.* (Working Paper No. 6691.) Washington, DC: National Bureau of Economic Research as cited in G. Hall, L.F. Quinn, & D.M. Gollnick (2008). *The joy of teaching.* Boston, MA: Pearson Education Inc.

4. Stronge, J. (2002). *Qualities of effective teachers.* Alexandria, VA: Association for Supervision and Curriculum Development.

5. See for instance researchers Powell, S.D. (2009). *An Introduction to Education.* Upper Saddle River, NJ: Pearson Education, Inc, (p. 324).

    Howsam, R. B., Corrigan, D.C., Denemark, G. W., & Nash, J.R. (1976). *Educating a profession.* Washington, DC: American Association of Colleges of Teacher Education.

    Ingersoll, R.(1997). *The status of teaching as a profession: 1900-1991.* Washington, DC: US Department of Education.

Rowan, B. (1994*).* Comparing teachers' work with work in other occupations: Notes on the profession of teaching. *Educational Researcher,* 23(6), 4 – 17, 21.

Web, L., Metha, A., & Jordan, K.E. (2007). *Foundations of American Education* (5th ed.). Upper Saddle River, NJ: Merrill/Prentice Hall as cited in S. D. Powell: An introduction to education. Upper saddle River, NJ: Pearson Education.

6.   Sadker, M. P. & Sadker, D. M. (2005). *Teachers, schools, and society.* (7th ed.). Boston, MA: McGraw Hill.

7.   Morrison, G. S. (2003). *Teaching in America.* Boston, MA: Pearson Education, Inc Periods.

Tomorrow's teachers: A report of the Holmes Group. East Lansing, MI (1986) as cite in   Sadker, M. P. & Sadker, D. M. (2005). Teachers, schools, and society. (7th ed.). Boston, MA: McGraw Hill.

8.   Carnegie forum on education and the economy, task force on teaching as a profession, *A Nation Prepared*: *Teachers for the 21st Century* . New York: Forum (1986) Sadker, M. P. & Sadker, D. M. (2005). Teachers, schools, and society. (7th ed.). Boston, MA: McGraw Hill.

9.   The Profession. (2008). Wikipedia. Retrieved from http://en.wikipedia.org/ wiki/Profession.

10. Sadker, M. P. & Sadker, D. M. (2005). *Teachers, schools, and society.* (7th ed.). Boston, MA: McGraw Hill, (p.16).

11. The National Board for Professional teaching standards. Retrieved from http://www.nbpts.org/the_standards/the_five_core_proposition Periods.

12. Center for Teaching quality. (2010). Retrieved from www.teachingquality. org/tsnbct Periods.

13.   Code of Ethics. (2008). Retrieved fromhttp://www.geocities.com/ pan_ andrew/teachers.htm Periods.

14. Howe, K. R. (1996, May, June). A conceptual basis for ethics in teacher education, Journal of Teacher Education, 37 in S. D. Powell (2009), An introduction to education. Upper Saddle River, NJ: Pearson Education. Inc. (p. 325).

15. Coates, D. E. (2006). *People skills training: Are you getting a return on your investment?* Retrieved from www.praxisconsulting.org/Peopleskills.pdf.

16. Morrison, G. S. (2003). *Teaching in America.* Boston: Allyn and Bacon. (p. 257).

17. Taylor. L. S. (2003). Only the brave should teach. (Pearl Buck) Retrieved from http://www.lewrockwell.com/taylor/taylor21.html Periods.

PHILOSOPHY AND HISTORY: THEY REALLY DO MATTER

Gereon Vaughn Methner teaches secondary French in Shawano Community Schools, Shawano, Wisconsin.

I knew I was taking a chance pursuing a foreign language degree because it seems that every decade schools change their approach— "shrink the curriculum" and reduce the importance of the subject I love to teach. Teaching French sounded like such a great idea when I entered college, but as student demographics change, its popularity has plunged in the public eye. I am constantly bombarded with students, parents, colleagues, and administrators who tell me the same thing, "It sounds like a neat language, but it's nowhere near as useful as Spanish." To this, I respond with somewhat of a deaf ear because French is spoken by over 100 million people around the world, namely our nearest neighbor, Canada. It is still the international language of diplomacy. It is also one of the languages that created English, therefore helping students to see the important connections between the French and English languages.

Consequently, I find myself questioning the usefulness of French, despite all the convincing arguments. It is disheartening to consider that something I have devoted so much of my time to could actually be deemed as useless. In the end, I always rely on my educational philosophy. I truly believe I am opening the minds of students who, under normal circumstances, would never have the opportunity to explore the French speaking world, and I am exposing them to that world, a world beyond their own. If I can encourage just one student to expand his or her world, gaining the rich experience of traveling as a result of my endless babble, then I've done my job.

LESSONS of the past shape our future. As a nation, we have grown to recognize and value a free, appropriate, compulsory education for all students. And as a nation, we ponder ageless philosophical questions regarding the overall purpose of education: Should children be educated to maintain the status quo, or should they be educated for the advancement of social change? Should schools focus on the basics, or should their focus be on an extended curriculum? Should schools be responsible for servicing the whole family or just the child? The combination of history and philosophy form the foundation upon which these questions are addressed. This chapter provides a brief history of schooling in America and discusses how philosophical views of education influence the teaching style in the classroom.

WHAT IS YOUR PHILOSOPHY OF EDUCATION?

The Greek word philosophy means "love and wisdom" and is merely a framework for examining age-old questions. Simply stated, beliefs about how students learn and what they should learn, forms the basis for a philosophy of education. Some of the age-old questions follow: Do students learn best from each other cooperatively, or through teacher interaction and lecture? Is it more important to focus on core concepts such as "readin', writin', and rithmatic," or should the curriculum be more broad? Should social justice be promoted in the classroom or left beyond the school door? These and other educational considerations grow out of who we are and our basic belief systems.

Three Main Branches of Philosophy

A deeper look into the study of philosophy involves the examination of the meaning of life (Metaphysics), the role of values and ethics in the classroom (Axiology), and how we know what we know (Epistemology).

Aristotle theorized that *Metaphysics* refers to looking beyond the physical world for the understanding of truth, reality, and our life purpose. Metaphysics addresses what is important to us, based on how we perceive the meaning of life. Do we control our destiny, or is it in the hands of a higher power? Is a child's ability up to us as educators, or is it largely determined beyond the classroom? Curricular choices are determined by what we know about reality. If you believe students require a specific knowledge base, the classroom focus will be on a certain subject matter. On the other hand, the student, not the subject matter, will be the centerpiece if the focus is more student-centered.[1]

Axiology concerns aesthetics and ethics. Aesthetics is the perception of beauty and ethics that morally guide our behavior. Questions of right and wrong, good or bad, beautiful or not, are value judgments. Schools promote value judgments and decide what is important through curriculum choices, through what is taught, and through ethical behavior expectations. Asking, "What is beauty or what is true?" will be answered in a dozen different ways. Teachers behave in accordance with their ethics, and parents who may not agree with the school's values, may choose an alternative environment such as home-schooling or a perhaps a non-public school.

Epistemology refers to how we know what we know and inquires, "What is knowledge?", "How is knowledge acquired?", "What do people know?", and "How do we know what we know?" [2] Epistemological decisions are made when curriculum standards determine what students need to know.[3] Morrison suggests five ways of knowing about the world:[4]

1. Knowing through experience—learning through our experiences and senses.

2. Knowing through authority—learning from authority figures such as parents, clergy, teachers, and written authority such as religious materials, government reports, and textbooks.

3. Knowing through logical reasoning—learning through *inductive reasoning* promotes critical thinking skills and problem solving, and learning through *deductive reasoning* promotes application to our existing constructs.

4. Knowing through intuition—learning through a combination of experiences, relationships, schooling, and the growth process.

5. Knowing through active construction—learning through activities both physical and mental, leading to new experiences that make sense of, and develop our understanding of the world.

THE INFLUENCE OF FIVE PHILOSOPHICAL ORIENTATIONS ON TEACHING STYLE

Many schools of thought influence classroom instructional practice. The five major philosophical schools of thought presented—Essentialism, Perennialism, Progressivism, Social Reconstructivism, and Existentialism illustrate two different instructional approaches—teacher-centered and student-centered.

Teacher-Centered Instruction

Essentialism and Perennialism are traditionally teacher-centered philosophies that focus on the essentials of academic knowledge and character development[5]. Classrooms are largely authoritarian, and instruction is typically not differentiated. A certain subject matter is crucial when transmitting traditional societal values from one generation to another.

Student-Centered Instruction

Progressivism, Social Reconstructionism, and Existentialism are student-centered philosophies concentrating on broadening the curriculum, making it relevant to students' lives. Within this philosophy, educating students for a desired, overall social change is a key focus for fostering critical thinking skills. In a student-centered classroom, instruction is differentiated to meet individual student learning styles.

The charts below illustrate characteristics of each of the five *Philosophical Orientations on Teaching Styles.*

TEACHER-CENTERED PHILOSOPHIES

Philosophy	Theorist Roots	Characteristics	School/Teacher Role
ESSENTIALISM (early 20th century) *Teacher/Subject Centered Philosophy*	William Bagley	Back to basics character development Resurgence with Sputnik launch Focus on: math, natural science, history, foreign language, literature	Transmit traditional moral values and intellectual knowledge to create model Does not promote: Vocational education, life-adjustment, watered-down content
PERENNIALISM (late 20th century) *Teacher/Subject Centered Philosophy*	Plato Aristotle Mortimer Adler St. Thomas Aquinas Robert Hutchins	Emphasize great books and time-tested ideas Humanities training Timeless understanding of human condition Truth is constant and unchanging	Transmit everlasting truths General course of study Rigorous curriculum Role model of values Direct Instruction

STUDENT-CENTERED PHILOSOPHIES

Philosophy	Theorist Roots	Characteristics	School/Teacher Role
PROGRESSIVISM (late 19th & 20th century) *Student-Centered Philosophy*	John Dewey	Citizenship education, Educational relevance Focus on: students' needs, change, and scientific method Inquiry learning, broadened curriculum, reduced influence with launch of Sputnik	Cultivate individuality based on student interest, abilities, and experiences Cooperative learning through experience and active play
SOCIAL RECONSTRUC-TIVISM (20th century) *Student-Centered Philosophy*	Theodore Brameld George Counts Paulo Freire	Addressing social questions to create a better society Focus on: social reform, preparing for a new social order Systems must be changed to overcome	Lead community based learning Assist in creating environment for change
EXISTENTIALISM (19th & 20th century) *Student-Centered Philosophy*	Jean Paul Sartre Soren Kierkegaard Friedrich Nietzsche A. S. Neill Maxine Greene	Respect for individualism No universal inborn nature Freely determine course Wide latitude for curricular choices	Sounding board to help student self-discovery Help students define their essence

These five Philosophical Orientations on Teaching Style are adapted from N. A. Paris. [5]

Developing a philosophy of education such as the five listed here, begins with thoughtful consideration of the ultimate purpose of education. How are "ways of knowing" to be established in instruction? What should be guiding our ethical and aesthetic considerations?   Is the classroom teacher-centered or student-centered? Authoritarian or non-authoritarian? Is the curriculum based on social action or basic skills? Historically, the purpose of education in the United States has mirrored democratic values and societal influences. The following pages offer a snapshot of historical events that have shaped our current educational thought. Schools do not operate in a vacuum, and whether the focus is on basic skills or social action, educational trends are cyclical and guided by societal needs.

The Colonial Period

The evolution of American education dates back to colonial times. Parents, often well-respected mothers, organized what were referred to as 'dame schools'. These early 17th century schools were loosely organized systems that gathered a handful of well-to-do children to read the Bible by candlelight in private homes. Young boys were often sent to participate in apprenticeship programs to learn a trade. Education was driven by religion, demonstrated by the Puritans who migrated to America pursuing religious freedom. Education, perceived as a path to heaven, consisted of reading, writing, and moral development—manners and social graces [6]. In 1642, the Massachusetts Bay Colony established the first thrust for all children to receive formalized instruction, and five years later, they began collecting taxes and appointing teachers.[7]

In an effort to promote the growth of education, Congress passed Land Ordinances in 1785 and 1787, designating that township land be reserved for public schools. Surprisingly, the Constitution of the United States provides no specific direction for the implementation of education. The Constitution does, however, provide power to each state, through the 10th Amendment. The power dictates that states must establish schools in the best interest of the state and its people.

The Common School

Schools in the 19th century typically served the rich until Horace Mann, a vocal proponent for schools for all socio-economic classes, created the first common school in the early 1820's in Massachusetts. Our current day elementary school had its beginning as a common school. Mann, who is considered to be the father of the common school, believed that schooling should be affordable to all and should assist in transforming the lower classes into a more educated workforce, encouraging everyone to become a contributing citizen. To make schools affordable to the lower classes, common schools of the 19th century were locally controlled and tax-dollar supported. This lead to the standardization of American education.

Mann firmly believed that students should be taught the basics of the Constitution to learn responsible, civic behavior. In addition, moral and ethical values, skills for everyday life, reading, writing, arithmetic, history, spelling, and geography were all to be components of the curriculum. Many leaders of the day such as Thomas Jefferson and Benjamin Franklin proposed that building an educated citizenry would promote a strong, democratic nation, and the common school seemed to fill that desire. Mann also believed much as we do today—that schools for the *common man* would help reduce the rising racial and social tension. However, this was not the case since many groups objected to the religious focus of the curriculum as well as the increased taxes to support such free schools. If this rhetoric sounds a bit familiar, it should. We continue to struggle with such principles to this very day. From these protests, we witnessed the dawn of private and parochial schools, as well as learning academies.[6] Although many did not believe such extended education was a necessity, a high school for boys was established in 1821 in Boston, and in 1852, for girls. Junior High schools were established in 1910 after the National Education Association *(NEA)* recommended that college preparatory classes should begin before high school. The NEA proved to be the pioneer in recommending that all students, poor and wealthy, take college preparatory courses.[7]

Immigration, Expansion and Compulsory Education

European immigration to America played a critical role in the growth of cities and the expansion of not only public education, but also the manufacturing and transportation industries. Even though public schools were tax supported, most poor families considered education a luxury, and instead sent their children into the workforce. States began passing compulsory education laws in 1852, the state of Massachusetts being at the forefront. [8] Compulsory education laws solved only part of the problem, so the federal government intervened and created laws restricting how much children were permitted to work in factories. In 1880, ten million or nearly 60% of the United States' white children were enrolled in elementary schools. [9]

Higher Education

Horace Mann is also credited with initiating the first push in the standardization of teacher training. Until the creation of the first teacher training program, males were the schoolmasters because women were perceived as incapable of instruction. In 1839, the first state-supported school for teacher training was again established in Massachusetts. These were termed "normal" schools and were two-year institutions designed to train women teachers. The curriculum covered history, philosophy, and teaching methods.[10] Normal schools became the career path for many women, and by the early 20th century, 71% of rural teachers were women .[11] Additionally, the Morrill Land Grant University Act of 1862 afforded each state 30,000 acres to create colleges of agriculture and mechanical education. [12] In response to the need for more highly trained teachers and a push for teacher professionalism, normal schools moved to four-year programs, and Masters Degrees developed in the 1930's and 1950's respectively.

The early 20th century was a period marked by Progressivism as the country was influenced by the writings of John Dewey. Progressive education changed the overall purpose of education—from subject-centered to more student-centered. The extended curriculum of the Progressive Movement considered the needs of the student in preparation for an ever-changing world.

In 1957, the Soviet Union launched Sputnik (the first satellite) into space, and that event changed the course of history. Fearing that the academic achievement of students in the United States was inferior, the Progressive Movement was quickly overtaken by a vigorously renewed focused on mastery of basic skills, namely in math and science.

The next five decades, marked by pivotal educational events affecting the education reform movements, are depicted in the chart below.[13]

1954	Brown vs. Board of Education ruled that separate but equal educational facilities are "inherently unequal"
1957-58	National Defense Education Act provided funds for science, math and foreign language in response to Sputnik
1965	Elementary and Secondary Education Act (ESEA of 1965) enacted programs such as Title I, bilingual education, and federal funds to help low-income students
1972	Title IX prohibited discrimination based on sex in schools
1975	Public Law 94-142 mandated a free, appropriate public education in the least-restrictive setting be provided for all handicapped children
1983	Release of *A Nation at Risk* called attention to the state of American public education leading to the beginning of pervasive reform efforts in public education
1980's	Standards Based Education Movement pushed for increased standards depicting content and performance based standards
1990's	School Choice Movement moved public schools to respond to market competition while addressing increased diversity in school populations Public Law 94-142 amended changing terminology from handicap to disability, adding autism, traumatic brain injury, and transitional services to the eligibility list
2001	No Child Left Behind reauthorized the ESEA of 1965 mandating measurable accountability standards through annual assessments, teacher qualifications, and sanctions for failing schools
2004	Individuals with Disabilities Education Improvement Act modified the individual education plan *(IEP)*, procedural safeguards, increased authority for school personnel in special education placement decisions, and alignment with the NCLB Act of 2001

The history of American education affects our present and future. The standards and accountability movement will likely color the educational landscape for decades to come. Historically the United States is in the midst of unprecedented reform efforts aimed at providing maximum opportunities for all children. There is perhaps no time in history where the educator's *philosophies of education* and instructional practices have to power to positively affect so many.

Chapter Activities

1. Consider your beliefs, values, and experiences and develop the components of your philosophy of education. Include your beliefs relative to:

    a. The three branches of philosophy

    b. The five philosophical orientations

    c. Purpose of education

    Provide examples of instructional practices illustrating your philosophy.

2. Identify what events in history have most influenced the course of American public education and explain whey you believe they were pivotal.

3. Think back to your high school teachers. Are you able to identify their philosophical orientations? What characteristics and behaviors lead to your conclusion?

Chapter Summary

1. The overall purpose of school is continually redefined based on the current needs of society. Pivotal historical events serve to shape the nation's educational focus.

2. A teacher's personal philosophy of education strongly influences instructional practices.

3. Beliefs relative to the three main branches of philosophy: metaphysics, axiology, and epistemology form the foundation of an educational philosophy.

4. Horace Mann, considered the father of the common school, is credited with creating schools for the *common man* to create an *educated citizenry*.

5. The Progressivism movement of the early 20th century was weakened by the launch of Sputnik in 1957.

Notes

1. Musial, D. (2005) as cited in G. Hall, L. Quinn & D. Gollnick (2008). *The joy of teaching. Boston*, MA: Pearson Education (p. 272).

2. Epistemology. Retrieved on November 28, 2008 from http://en.wikipedia. org/wiki/Epistemology.

3. Powell, S. D. (2009). *An introduction to education: Choosing your teaching path.* Upper Saddle River, NJ: Pearson Education.

4. Morrison, G. S. (2003). *Teaching in America.* Boston MA: Pearson Education (p. 351-2).

5. Paris, N.A. (n.d.) *Major educational philosophies.* Retrieved November 20, 2008 from http://ksuweb.kennesaw.edu/~nparis/educ7700 EDUCATIONAL%20 PHILOSOPHIES%20(Major)_.doc.

6. Sadker, M. P. & Sadker, D. M. (2005). *Teachers, schools, and society* (7th ed.). Boston, MA: McGraw Hill.

7. Hall, G. E., Quinn, L. F. & Gollnick, D.M. (2008). *The joy of teaching.* Boston, MA: Pearson Education, Inc.

8. Koch, J. (2009) *So you want to be a teacher: Teaching and learning in the 21st century.* Boston, MA: Houghton Mifflin Company (p. 64).

9. Sadker, M. P. & Sadker, D. M. (2005). *Teachers, schools, and society* (7th ed.). Boston, MA: McGraw Hill (p. 294).

10. Koch, J. (2009) *So you want to be a teacher: Teaching and learning in the 21st century.* Boston, MA: Houghton Mifflin Company (p. 68).

11. Hoffman, N. (1981) as cited in J. Koch (2009) *So you want to be a teacher: Teaching and learning in the 21st century.* Boston, MA: Houghton Mifflin Company (p. 68).

12. Morrison, G. S. (2003). *Teaching in America.* Boston MA: Pearson Education (p. 333).

13. American Educational History: A Hypertext Timeline. Retrieved on November 10, 2008 from http://C:/Documents%20and%20Settings/_ HP_Administrator /My%20Documents/Chalk%20Talk/ American %20 Educational%20History%20Timeline.htm.

Classroom Management: It's not Rocket Science

CLASSROOM MANAGEMENT: FIRST YEAR STYLE

Kathy Solomon is a third grade teacher as Golbow Elementary in Katy Independent School District, a suburb of Houston, Texas

Classroom management was the last thing I considered when setting up my first classroom. Fresh from college, I thought I had everything I needed: great lesson plans, cute bulletin boards and a positive attitude. All through student teaching and my graduate school internships, I relied on others to set up their management aspect. There was always a system in place, and I went with that system. Simple—Right? I really had never had to create one on my own.

My first year of teaching was a challenging one. I taught third grade in a Title I school in a suburb of Houston, and I had three students in my class who were already on a BIP (behavior intervention plan). I had always heard the saying, "Don't let them see you smile until December." But I thought that surely my class will be different; I'd show them that I understood, and they'd listen to me more. Looking back, I can't believe how I thought that was going to happen without laying some important groundwork.

I never thought of myself as a pushover, but in the beginning I felt just awful if a student became mad, disappointed, or worse – cried! I constantly gave warnings, and it didn't take students long to figure out that most of the time my threats were empty. Kids are smart – given the chance they will try and manipulate their teachers. By the end of September I wised up and gave them marks (they had conduct cards) after only one warning, but I realized I was still very inconsistent. For example, if a student always had his/her homework, I would let one missing assignment slide, but others I would mark. Students who never got into fights were overlooked when they argued, while others might be sent to the office. These double-standards proved problematic. When the rest of the students caught on, I heard, "But you didn't care when SHE didn't clean up after herself!" or "No fair!! HE didn't get in trouble when HE yelled out!"

My advice to you is this: while you don't have to start out mean, you must start out consistent, and with a smile. Now in my second year, I still work on my classroom management. While I've gotten better, there is still room for improvement. There are so many things I wish I would've known—the time and energy I could've saved! Don't let those big eyes and pleading smiles get the best of you!

KATHY'S story may be similar to many novice teachers. Maybe you too, have been told somewhere along the line that you should not smile until November, and even that smiling was a sin or a sign of weakness. We don't know about you, but we cannot envision having a teacher who did not smile! Perhaps you can imagine a teacher or two who practiced that to the letter. You can be sure that memories of "frowners" do not evoke feelings of affection. Contrary to what you may have heard, it does not have to be synonymous with a lack of classroom control. As a matter of fact, if you remember back to some of your favorite teachers, they smiled AND maintained a well-managed classroom. Smiling is an important human behavior and assists in creating a comfortable, safe, classroom community.

By the end of this chapter, you will be equipped with the tools to create a well- managed classroom….with a smile! The information presented here is not rocket science by any stretch of the imagination. This information steals the best ideas from those who know how to get the job done. In addition to consulting the talented folks referenced here, there are a multitude of websites and resources that provide useful information on managing your classroom. The principles presented here, we believe, can be applied and modified for use in any classroom by any teacher at any time. As you prepare to embark on that first classroom of shining, inquisitive, and sometimes challenging faces, please keep in mind that *if you cannot manage your classroom, you cannot be an effective teacher.* Ryan and Cooper describe classroom management as "the set of teacher behaviors that create and maintain conditions in the classroom permitting instruction to take place efficiently and effectively".[1] In the following chapter, we endeavor not to hammer you over the head, or to scare you to death, but instead, to provide you an overview of the what we feel will encourage to get on the right foot from the first minute of your first day of your exciting new teaching career.

Creating an Environment for Learning

Part of the preparation process is learning how to create a classroom conducive to success. Successful classrooms are those that promote learning achievement through the consideration of physical, organizational, sociological, political, economic and cultural factors.[2] Morrison notes a healthy, positive classroom climate is the atmosphere created through:

- [ ] your positive beliefs about teaching and learning

- [ ] the manner in which you value the culture and beliefs of your students

- [ ] your belief in your students' ability to achieve

- [ ] the manner in which you interact with students and peers

- [ ] your quality of instruction

- [ ] your consideration of your students' learning styles

- [ ] the degree to which teacher, students, and school have shared values and common goals

- [ ] your classroom organization

- [ ] your classroom management procedures[3]

ORGANIZATION: THE FIRST LINE OF DEFENSE

There is a famous sign that reads, "A cluttered desk is the sign of a clear mind." Many of us can relate to this comment. But the problem is ....all we can see is the cluttered desk! Sometimes a teacher's desk may resemble organized confusion. While this may work for some people, it might be nice to actually see what color the top of your desk is from time to time. Also consider that you are setting the example for your students. Is your desk the message you want to send? The following paragraphs offer some suggestions to assist in organizing your room or area. You may choose these or create your own personal systems. How you choose to organize your classroom is ultimately your preference; what matters is that you have a system that works for you!

Paper vs. Machine

Even though we have moved into a world guided by technology, it still may be a good rule of thumb for teachers to get a desk calendar. Some businesses provide them free to teachers. Technology is a wonderful tool, but in the classroom situation, nothing takes the place of a large desk calendar that can remind you of things at a glance. You can quickly organize yourself with due dates for lesson plans, bus and hall duty, upcoming extracurricular events, and staff meetings. No one, especially during the first few years, wants to forget a meeting or a date for requested paperwork that is due in to the office. A desk calendar can aid in relieving the pressures of recalling day-to-day events.

Many of us use mobile devices as calendars, datebooks, and appointments and for just about everything else nowadays. But having your phone, Blackberry, or PDA out and about in the classroom may not be the best idea or role model. Another way the calendar may come in handy is for your daily class agenda.

While teachers can't predict what each day will bring, you can use a calendar to organize a timeframe when units of specific information will be covered. This way, you can get a feel for the time you have been given in a quarter or semester. By plotting out how long each unit will take, you can make sure you set time aside for each topic. It serves as a great overview of the semester, while also making sure all subjects are covered. Additionally, it will provide a wonderful chronology of your first year, one you will look back on fondly for years to come.

While calendars are a good way to start your organization, having an adequate filing system is probably the second most important feature. Most organizations are understandably "going green," but you will still have your share of paperwork that can pile up very quickly. Between the office, your local teachers' union, authentic assessment student work samples, and your own teaching, you will be amazed at how rapidly a small forest will accumulate in your room! One of the keys to an organized filing system is utilizing a filing cabinet. Do not laugh; some classrooms do not have any! If you walk into your room and see no filing cabinet, ask your building engineer (others may call them custodians) if one is available. If not, then you will need to be creative. Xerox boxes and hanging file folders can be useful as a temporary replacement for the actual cabinet.

The next step you need to take is to decide how to file your information. Many teachers use file folders as a way to keep units and other information separated. Folders are a great way of keeping small pieces of information available at a moment's notice. If you choose to use folders, you may want to use varying colors to better separate the subject matter, especially if you are teaching multiple preps. Of course, you can also divide the preps into different drawers of the cabinet, completely separating the material.

Another route to consider is one that many teachers are now using: the three-ring binder. There is one binder for each subject or prep you teach. Binders are available in a wide array of colors. They can be labeled on the outside, making them clear, simple, and easily accessible. Binders make it easy to organize unit plans, worksheets, supplemental information, and previous quizzes and tests. When you are planning your semester or quarter, in a binder you can view the whole course, rather than pulling each individual file one by one. It has saved teachers a lot of time and space. You could locate the binders directly beside lesson plan books and all other material you need for teaching.

If you are teaching multiple periods or subjects each day, it is helpful to make sure that the homework and graded materials are located in a central spot. Oftentimes, teachers use plastic shelving units to organize materials. These shelves are useful for collecting graded homework, bell work, or to collect papers throughout the day. They can be marked in any manner, such as "inbox" or "graded" box. Students can then feel free to hand in materials saving you time in collecting. After students hand it in the proper slot, it will be right there for you to retrieve at your convenience. At the end of the period or day, you can gather the material to be graded, record the grades, and return it to the "graded" box. Accordingly, this diminishes time spent returning material to students.

However, be aware that these boxes should be located near your desk to avoid tampering by students.

Strategize & Maximize

Teachers must consider organizational strategies to maximize time. If secondary teachers' organizational strategies are not carefully planned, their already abbreviated instructional time could consist of half their class period. It is essential to create classroom systems that eliminate wasting precious instructional time on tasks such as: taking attendance/lunch count, gathering materials, book order money, parent notes and permission slips, and reviewing missed assignments for returning students. Valuable time can be lost to these tasks. Consider that these tasks take 12 minutes per day x 60 minutes per week, 240 minutes per month, and 2,160 minutes (36 hours) in a year. Lost instructional time is a real consideration in these days of accountability and may be something closely observed by your supervisor. Harry Wong,[4] veteran teacher and author, notes that many of these essential daily tasks can be completed while students are engaged in bell work at the beginning of the day. Bell work is a vital classroom tool and will be discussed in greater detail in the classroom management section.

While students are busy with bell work, utilizing a seating chart allows attendance to be taken quickly as well as tracking of daily assignments for students returning to school. Students can then place notes, lunch money, book orders, etc... in pre-established locations for collection. One suggestion that works well for some teachers is to cut a paper plate in half for each student. Staple it to a board with the student's name or picture. Then upon entering the room, students can drop items in their paper plate folder. Another idea is to tape a folder to the front of each student's desk. It is easy to circulate and collect items in a quiet and orderly manner. Whatever system you decide to use, make sure it is organized in a way that information can be easily obtained. The job of educating students is complex enough. A well-organized room can minimize confusion, allowing you to concentrate on the real task at hand, *teaching*.

Preparation is a Virtue

Preparation cannot be stressed enough. The key is to plan for all the variables that you can control before school begins. Wong[5] asserts that "readiness is the primary determinant of teacher effectiveness". While we veteran teachers remember that incredibly strong urge to beautify our room to the nines the first day, it is important to spend the lion's share of your preparation time on tasks related to classroom management. Wong recommends not over-decorating at the expense of losing time on the larger organizational issues. Do not worry if there is a bare bookshelf, a plain bulletin board, or learning center undone—no one will notice. However, it will be noticeable if on the first day if you have not used ample time to think through your procedures and management strategies.

Below is a list of items in which you may want to consider. The list is by no means exhaustive, and you will surely have your own to add.

- ❏ Acquire a copy of the school's handbook and policies; read it from cover to cover

- ❏ Familiarize yourself with the district's web site. It may be a great way to refer parents for information

- ❏ Familiarize yourself with the school/grounds and the most expedient entrances/exits

- ❏ Familiarize yourself with the school's emergency procedures; clearly post them

- ❏ Prepare and organize supplies making sure they are at your fingertips

- ❏ Check with the office to make sure you have all necessary forms: school procedures, lunch attendance, academic standards, etc...)

- ❏ Test your equipment/software to make sure all is working (SMART Board, PowerPoint, etc...)

- ❏ Post as much information as possible: name/room number or section/ period on door, discipline plan, procedures, daily schedules, etc...

- ❏ Post objectives, class assignments, homework and upcoming events (secondary teachers especially)

- ❏ Prepare bulletin boards—Harry Wong suggests an "All about me" board to help students know you better—leave one board free for student work

- ❏ Prepare seat assignments, nametags, etc...

- ❏ Make sure the office has a copy of your behavior management plan

- ❏ Organize your students' desks for ease of circulation— it is harder to misbehave with the teacher near

- ❏ Plan a space for your students' belongings—elementary and secondary students' needs vary

- ❏ Make sure you have reviewed all your teaching materials— and in a word: OVERPLAN

- ❏ Create a space for "time out" or buddy up with colleague to create a "time out" area for students (not on the first day of course—but it must be part of your plan)

- ❏ Have a camera ready to take pictures the first week of school for use: bulletin boards, parent night activities, etc...

❏ Keep an appointment calendar in view to remind you of important meetings, assemblies, special events, and/or duties (bus, hall, and cafeteria)

Knowing that you have covered your bases will help you to build confidence. With confidence comes competence.

Respect is the Name of the Game

Classroom management begins and ends with seven little letters: R-E-S-P-E-C-T. Just like Aretha Franklin says, "Find out what it means to me." Everyone wants respect. While the word "respect," may be a vague or variable term, it is most effective if it can be concretely defined for use in your classroom. When present, respect is purposeful, and with its presence, authentic learning is more likely to flourish.

Respect, however, must be mutual. Often, teachers believe they deserve respect based simply on their classroom leadership position. Ellen Kronowitz writes "Modeling respect in your classroom is the most important thing you can do to establish a classroom community based on democratic values." [2] Respect is a two-way street. You have to give it to get it. And a democratic, respectful classroom creates an atmosphere where disruptions are less likely to occur. To students of any age, mutual respect between teachers and students could be the difference between success and failure.

A Bit of Common Sense Goes a Long Way

Now, do not delude yourself. This is not a cake walk. Even in the most well-meaning, respectful classrooms, problems arise. Before we discuss some specific research relative to maintaining an effective classroom, there are some *common sense* rules in which all teachers should try to adhere.

1. Do not escalate the problem by causing confrontation. Psychiatrist and educator Rudolf Dreikurs theorized that the four goals of misbehavior are to:

   i. Gain attention

   ii. Exercise power

   iii. Exact revenge

   iv. Avoidance of failure (feelings of inadequacy).

   Students first misbehave because they desire attention. If they do not receive the attention they seek, whether good or bad (e.g. performing well on an assignment or throwing a tantrum), they move onto seeking power (e.g. they may refuse to complete an assignment). If their power struggle is not satisfied, they seek revenge. If even revenge does not achieve the desired response, they begin to feel inadequate.[3] Teachers, novice and veteran, often find themselves in a power struggle with a student before they know it. Be aware of that on the second— "Oh, yes you did". You are now officially in a no-win power struggle with the rest of the class as anxious onlookers watching your classroom control erode. Being confrontational with students only causes a negative, *survival mode* reaction. Never allow the situation to escalate until the student is out of control. Keep these tips in mind to prevent a "bad to worse" situation:

❑ Keep your voice low and even (do not increase rate of speech) and remain calm

❑ Refrain from confrontational body language (crossing arms, standing too close—stand diagonally instead of facing head-on)

❑ Be the adult, and stay on the topic of the misbehavior—disregard irrelevant information (students will try to "egg" you on with non-relevant data—ignore it)

❑ Keep the environment free from possible peril (create accessible desk patterns, keep sharp objects out of harms way, separate students who are engaging negatively)

❑ Remind students of rules, give choices, and adhere to your classroom limits

2. Try to identify the emotions behind the misbehavior and whether they are seeking attention, power, or revenge. While it is not always possible to ascertain *why* a student misbehaves, it is often easier for you to respond appropriately if you know the source. It may not be you. It could be a home situation, a dispute with a best friend, or an issue on the bus ride to school. Offering a helping hand or a listening ear can be an amazing tool. Many students do not think teachers care about their lives. When you demonstrate you truly care, their respect for you will increase.

3. Talk to the student away from the rest of the class. Do not cause a scene; sometimes a stage is exactly the kind of revenge (feelings of inadequacy) the student seeks. Call the student to the back of the room, and quietly discuss what is bothering him/her. Again, do not make this an opportunity for a power struggle to public display.

4. Create connections between home and school. Never allow the first communication between you and home to be on the day the student misbehaves in your class. Prevent these uncomfortable and unprofessional first meetings by communicating, in some way, with parents before problems arise. Sending a letter home, or making a quick "hello" call at the beginning of the school year can go a very long way in building supportive relationships between school and home. This is also a great opportunity to introduce a pathway for communication. Explain your classroom structure, and you will have a much better chance establishing mutual expectations

with the students' parents or guardians. Subsequently, when you may have to contact the home at a later date, perhaps maybe to discuss an unpleasant situation, you have already created positive communication upon which to draw.

5.   Thomas R. McDaniel, described eleven techniques for better classroom discipline in a 1986 article in Phi Delta Kappan titled, "A Primer on Classroom Discipline: Principles Old and New" [4] These eleven techniques are described below:

a. *Focusing*

Focusing refers to gaining everyone's attention before you begin. It means that you will not start until everyone has settled down. Often new teachers believe that students will stand at attention once they begin teaching. This may work sometimes, but typically you will have to ensure that the conversation taking place in the corner of the room, and the note-passing off to the left corner cease before you begin. Gain their attention, and then highlight this expectation by waiting an additional three to five seconds after the classroom is completely quiet. Speak in a normal, regular tone. A soft spoken teacher is likely to have a calmer, quieter classroom that is more focused.

b. *Direct Instruction*

Direct instruction is very effective for keeping students' attention through the employment of clear lesson expectations and active involvement. During *direct instruction,* the teacher begins by detailing exactly what she and the students will be doing for the entire class period, setting time limits for each task. Activities are varied and engaging, and students may find it harder to "wander" when they know they must keep deadlines. Techniques may include: student recitation in unison, board work, and reading round-robin style around the room. A few incentives follow: "We may have some time at the end of the period for you to work on your homework, read your favorite book, or go to the music corner if we can complete our lesson activities". The students soon realize that the more time they waste, the less time they will have to engage in their own desired activities at the end of the period.

c. *Monitoring*

Perhaps the most effective tool in maintaining a well-controlled classroom is to be out there *monitoring* them. Make your rounds in the room, intermittently checking students' work. Your first sweep verifies that all have effectively initiated the task. Your second round, after their initial engagement in the task, allows you to be proactive, checking that key components are being followed, and answering questions, as well as providing individualized assistance.

When you are out and about in the room, students are more likely to begin the task when requested which, in turn, diminishes misbehavior and makes your monitoring easier.

d. Modeling

"Values are caught, not taught." Teachers need to *model* the behaviors they wish to see. Forget the old "Do as I say, not as I do" song. If you want students to be kind, polite, timely, engaged, organized, and in control, then they should see those behaviors exhibited by you, their teacher. You cannot disregard papers on the floor, speak rudely, give discourteous responses, yell, invade the personal space of others and then expect your students to aspire a higher standard. They *must* see you model desirable behaviors first and foremost.

e. Non-verbal Cueing

This very useful strategy ensures that you can keep attention while losing the least amount of class time. Your *non-verbal cues* can be whatever works for you as long as its meaning is clear and established. Some teachers use turning the light off and on, tapping a bell, hand clapping, and facial expressions. Other uses include touching a student's shoulder, redirecting attention by lightly tapping a finger on the correct page, and standing next to a student during a lesson. Non-verbal cues can also include hand gestures, facial expressions, and body posture. It is essential that the cues chosen for your room *work* for you and have clear meaning to the students.

f. Environmental Control

Creating an inviting, upbeat, interesting environment is very important. Remember that students can be distracted with too much, but appropriate color and lighting is important to environment control, and routine changes of scenery are also necessary. You can have areas that are more active, and others that are quiet, calm and subdued depending on the activity.   In addition, students can bring items from home such as pictures or past projects for which they are proud. Harry Wong suggests creating a "Personality Board" [5] that allows students to learn more about you as person; as they get to know you better, you may see fewer problems with discipline simply for the sheer fact that you are genuinely sharing with them a piece of yourself. Items for a personality board, Wong suggests, might include your diploma, your past grade cards, pictures, awards, hobbies, favorite sports, places traveled, and pet pictures.

g. Low-profile Intervention

Much like non-verbal cuing, *low-profile intervention* helps to prevent situations from escalating by providing a quiet, calm negotiation time whenever possible without interrupting the flow of the lesson. In other words, *do not use a hammer when a feather will suffice.* Effective teachers try to anticipate problems and are careful not to reward misbehavior by allowing it to become the focus of attention. Some examples of low-profile intervention include the use of *name-dropping* during lecturing. To illustrate: a student is talking or is off task— his/her name can be cleverly dropped seamlessly into the dialogue. "You can probably see, Angela, how an adjective is used in this sentence to…" Just upon hearing her name and keeping it a low-profile, Angela is refocused on the task, and the momentum of the class is uninterrupted.

h. Humanistic I-messages

Thomas Gordon, creator of Teacher Effectiveness Training, [6] suggests the use of a technique called *Humanistic I-Messages.* This relays to the student the effect their behavior has on the teacher and the classroom as a whole. The technique includes three parts: 1. Description of the student's behavior 2. Effect of the behavior, and 3. Emotions evoked within the teacher. For example, "Why don't you start your work when you are asked? I have to take more time with you, and then I have less time to spend with other students; that truly frustrates me." Gordon suggests this emotionally compelling statement made by the frustrated teacher: "I cannot imagine what I have done to you that I do not deserve the respect from you that I get from the others in this class. If I have been rude to you or inconsiderate in any way, please let me know. I feel as though I have somehow offended you, and now you are unwilling to show me respect." If you deliver your reprimand within an "I statement", you have a better chance prompting a modification of behavior with that student instantaneously.

i. Positive Discipline

Much like it connotes, *positive discipline* focuses on the use of language that states the students' privileges as well as consequences. This is used effectively in classroom rules that clearly describe the expectations within the classroom. For example, "Move through the building in an orderly manner.", instead of "No-running in the room.", "Settle conflicts appropriately", instead of "No fighting.", "Leave gum at home.", instead of "No gum chewing." Praising the desired behavior a student exhibits is an important component of positive discipline.

j. Assertive Discipline

Assertive discipline is a democratic system for setting limits and empowering students in the classroom. This system created by Lee Canter asserts that the teacher is the authority in the classroom, and no student has the right to interfere with the learning of other students in the class. Canter's style of classroom management, which is explored in more detail in the next section, encourages the use of rewards, clear rules and concise, consistent consequences. This classroom management philosophy creates students who learn the ability to make appropriate choices and will hopefully self-regulate their own behavior.

k. Assertive I-messages

A little different than Humanistic I-Messages, *Assertive I-Messages* are statements that the teacher uses in an assertive discipline classroom when dealing with a misbehaving student. The statements are clear and detail precisely the students' obligations. For example, "I want you to replace the book and return to your seat," or "I need you to pick up that pencil and apologize to Karen," or "I expect you to take out your paper and write your name." Because of inexperience, a novice teacher might say, "I want you to stop that," which may initiate confrontation, argument, and denial. Because the focus is on the inappropriate behavior, the student is quick to respond, "I wasn't doing anything!" or "It wasn't my fault..." or "Since when is there a rule against..." and then the escalation has begun. Again, remember to state your I-message so that it is focused on the desired behavior you wish to see demonstrated and not the negative.

Words from the Experts

The recommendations presented in this section focus on the writings of Harry Wong and Lee Canter, both of which provide practical, common sense approaches to managing your classroom. Harry Wong's book *The First Days of School* [5] is a resource worth perusing, and some of his most compelling points will be presented here. Both researchers strongly suggest putting in considerable time during the first days and weeks of school to create a well-managed classroom. Yes, we know this is hard. While your peers are heading full force into teaching the curriculum, you will be spending a substantial part of your day establishing rules and routines, rewarding appropriate behavior, and teaching and re-teaching the acceptable behaviors in your classroom. If it is any comfort, and it certainly should be, be assured that more intense attention to classroom management issues during the early weeks will pay off. Then, you will sail through the rest of the year in a well-oiled, more productive learning environment. Accordingly, you will be less likely to fall prey to the number one reason causing novice teachers to leave teaching in the first two years: issues related to behavior management.

Lee Canter's Assertive Discipline [7] is a systematic approach to a democratic behavior management system that promotes empowering students to self-regulate their actions, hence better equipping them in making positive choices. Assertive discipline supposes there is no acceptable reason for misbehavior, so teachers must respond quickly and consistently to students' inappropriate actions. Canter also asserts that in establishing acceptable behavior in the classroom, students should not have to guess what you expect. As an assertive teacher, you must "clearly and firmly communicate the classroom expectations and be prepared to reinforce words with appropriate actions." [6] To establish an assertive classroom, it is essential that the teacher adhere to three essential steps. First you much teach the behavior you want to see. Remember… your idea of being "quiet" will probably have different interpretations to each student If you have a preferred "listening position" or an idea of a "straight line," or want students to "come prepared to class", then it is important that you teach your class what you mean specifically. Secondly, students must be afforded varied opportunities to practice the appropriate behaviors you are expecting. This will ensure that everyone knows again, what the expectations are. Canter suggests that you practice, practice, and practice the behaviors you want to permeate the classroom. Ample practice in the beginning means less reminding throughout the year. Lastly, you as the teacher must generously offer praise and rewards for the appropriate behaviors when they are demonstrated. Often undesirable behaviors will disappear by merely praising exemplary behavior. According to Harry Wong, if you do not have a plan, you are planning to fail.[5] Please remember that your tone and actions on the first minute of the first day of school will set the tone for rest of the year. Students naturally want to push the ticket. If you keep a level head, be the authority in your classroom, show respect, and maintain open communication, you will find the problems other teachers tackle may not occur in your room quite as often.

Procedures and Routines

Wong [5] contends that the majority of classroom misbehavior is caused by the failure of teachers to establish clear procedures and routines for students. A procedure is "simply a method or process for how things are to be done in the classroom", and routines are what students do automatically without being told." *Procedures* become habitual *routines* with practice. Wong further notes that training students to follow your procedures begins on the first day. It is your responsibility to set the tone by greeting your students at the door with a smile, directing them to their assigned seats, and alerting them to the bell/work on the board. Bellwork is an essential component of any effective classroom. Providing work to be completed upon entering the room conveys the message that you care enough to be prepared for them. This then, will be the dawn of a day stocked full of non-stop learning activities. Equally important, there is no *down-time* in an effective classroom. By being prepared to infuse each moment with engaged learning, you will be ready and waiting to meet those eager faces. Thus you will create an environment conducive to success.

The Plan

A discipline plan has three parts: rules, positive recognition, and consequences.

Most experts agree that there should be no more than five classroom rules, and students should take an active role in their development. Canter suggests choosing rules…

a. that will let students know what behaviors are expected at all times

b. that are observable (stay away from vague concepts such as "good, behave, and polite" as they are hard to define and difficult to enforce)

c. that can be applied at all times throughout the day

d. that apply to behavior only; they should not involve academic functioning

Rules, Rewards and Consequences

As one of the final, but major components of your classroom management plan, make certain the rules, consequences, and rewards are clearly posted in your room. They should be reviewed often until all students are familiar with expectations as well as rewards and consequences for behavior. You should note that your rewards need not be huge, expensive productions. A reward, many times, is simply something that a student earns that someone else did not. A trip to your local bargain basement can provide inexpensive tangible rewards, if you choose, and your creativity can take care of the rest. For instance, consider the following rewards if you are teaching younger students: marbles in a jar, VIP certificate, stickers and stamps, pencils, positive calls to parents, name in newsletter, first in line, teacher helper, and popcorn while working quietly. Secondary teachers may consider positive calls home, additional time with a favorite computer task, chewing gum or enjoying a drink for the period (with permission from administration), homework pass, opportunities to choose seatwork, music, lunch with teacher, school-wide recognition board, mention in morning announcements, or sitting with friend for a week. All students, big and small, (and we, as well) enjoy a smile, word of encouragement, or additional attention from a respected individual.

As a general rule, it is inadvisable to allow punishments to "carryover" from one class day to another. "Wiping the slate clean" as much as possible allows for a positive approach to the next class meeting. If a student continues to be held under a "cloud" of previous missteps, what motivation is there to try to improve? Surely you would not want to be constantly reminded of a misdeed over the morning announcements each day for a week, when all you want is a "do-over". Allow your students the dignity and confidence to have that "do-over". You will not be disappointed.

Classroom Rules	Classroom Rules
Follow rules the first time they are given	Be in class on time
Raise your hand for permission to speak	Keep your hands, feet, and other objects to yourself
Raise your hand for permission to leave your seat	Listen to instructions the first time they are given
Do not touch anyone else with your hands, your feet or any object	Have all materials ready to use when the bell rings
No cursing or profanity	Be in seat when bell rings
Wait for directions with no talking	Bring all books and materials to class
Eyes in front when teacher is talking	No personal grooming during class time
Change tasks quickly and quietly	Sit in your assigned seat daily
Complete morning routine	Follow directions the first time they are given
Report directly to the assigned area	No cursing or teasing
	Stay in your seat unless directed to do otherwise

Rewards		Rewards
Individual	**Class-wide**	Praise
Stickers	Party	Positive notes home (random)
Notes and calls home	Movie	Whole-in class weekly free choice music time
Visit to principal	Treats Lunch in classroom	"Raise a grade" coupon (monthly)
	Extra Recess	"Good as Gold" Raffle ticket (semester)
		Movie and Popcorn party (semester)
		Selective rewards throughout year

Consequences or Penalties	Consequences or Penalties
If you choose to break a rule:	Name on board = 10 minutes detention at lunch hour
First Time: Name on board. Warning	One check = 20 minutes detention at lunch hour
Second Time: One check. 15 minutes after school	Two checks = 30 minutes detention at lunch hour and a call home
Third Time: Two checks. minutes after school.	Three checks = entire lunch detention, home called and a trip to the office
Fourth Time: Three checks. 45 minutes after school. Parents called	
Fifth Time: Four checks. 60 minutes after school, referral written and student sent to office.	**Consequences**
Severe Disruption: Student sent immediately to office	Demerit or Detention Write ways to correct problem Being last to leave Deprivation of some reward Exclusion from class participation
Names and checks erased each Thursday.	

Source : Sample Plans (Harry Wong)

Now that we've discussed *Rules, Rewards, and Consequences*, we will look at a sample breakdown of the discipline plan presented by Harry K. Wong in the book, *The First Days of School* (1991). This table visually divides the three categories of the discipline plan as mentioned: classroom rules, rewards, and consequences.

Lee Canter suggests that moving toward a well-managed classroom should include:

❑ Developing a solid sense of trust and R-E-S-P-E-C-T

❑ Teaching students how they are expected to behave in your classroom

❑ Establishing a discipline plan that provides structure and identifies behavior limits

❑ Teaching the discipline plan to students

❑ Preparing to carry out positive and negative consequences

❑ Dealing with disruptive behavior quickly, consistently, and effectively

A Final Thought

Effective classrooms are those where the teacher is prepared, the students are engaged and mutual respect abides. Affirmative behavior is maintained by establishing structure, consistency, and by procedures that are clearly delineated, rehearsed and reinforced. Teaching is your chosen profession—and it is the most noblest of choices. Make your day, week, month, year and career the best it can be with a well- managed well-maintained classroom.

Chapter Activities

Activity one

Creating a Classroom Management Plan

In a group of future teachers planning to teach a similar grade level, create a working behavior plan for your classroom. Present your plan to your peers.

Age/Grade Level   **Subject**

Classroom Rules: 1.

2.

3.

4.

5.

Rewards:

Consequences:

Room set-up specifics:

Activities to explain, rehearse, and reinforce rules:

Activity Two

Read through, and then choose one of the "Behavior Vignettes" below. Then address each of the three points while considering your chosen vignette:

1. Identify the target behavior on which you will focus (What are they currently doing and what do you want them to do?)

2. Discuss what you perceive may be the goal of the misbehavior and why?

3. Provide 2 - 3 suggestions for modifying the behavior within the classroom: Your plan of action

Behavior Vignettes

(Middle Elementary)

An 8 year-old boy in 3rd grade is constantly out of his seat while you are instructing, and during seat assignments he cannot initiate tasks because he always has questions regarding the directions related to the task.

(Upper Elementary)

You are a music teacher, and a 6th grade class repeatedly acts out and instigates disputes with each other while in your class. So far, they have not completed any of the lessons you have planned for them. You are at your wits end.

(Secondary)

A 10th grade student continually waits until the bell rings before she gets to her seat, even though she is aware of the rule to be in her seat when the bell rings.

(Middle School)

A 7th grader is consistently late in arriving to his first period class and does not turn in homework. He is very quiet and does not interact much with other students.

(Lower Elementary)

During your first grade PE class, three of the students are constantly horsing around and not following directions.

(Secondary)

An 11th grade male student constantly talks out in class, often with smart remarks, and waits for his classmates to laugh.

(Middle School)

In your 7th grade math class, you notice one girl in the class who turns in 1 of 4 homework assignments. You have already made her aware that she is missing points, but the situation has not improved.

(Secondary)

During your senior level chemistry class, you notice that during group work, which is a mandatory component of the class, you have a group where one student is always horsing around, and other students are really becoming tired of it.

Chapter Summary

1.   Effective classroom management is essential for successful instruction.

2.   Assertive Discipline is a systematic approach to democratic behavior management that promotes empowering students to regulate their actions.

3.   Inappropriate classroom behavior is caused from a lack of procedures and routines.

4.   Teachers should model the behaviors they wish to see in their student's exhibit.

5.   Never engage in a power struggle with a student.

6.   Considerable time should be afforded in the first weeks of school to establish a well-managed classroom.

7.   Creating an environment for learning begins with a healthy, positive classroom climate with consideration for physical, sociological, political, economic, cultural and organizational factors.

8.   Preparation, readiness, and organization are the primary determinates of teacher effectiveness.

9.   New teachers should get a copy of the school's handbook and policies and read it from cover to cover.

Notes

1.   Ryan, K. and Cooper (2007). *Those who can, teach* (11th ed.). Boston: Houghton Mifflin. (p. 499) as cited in Janice Koch (2009). *So you want to be a teacher*. Boston: Houghton Mifflin.

2.   Johnson, S. M. (1990). Teachers at work: Achieving success in our schools. New York: Basic Books as cited in G. S. Morrison *Teaching in America*. (p.16) Boston: Allyn and Bacon.

3.   Morrison, G. S. (2003). *Teaching in America*. Boston: Allyn and Bacon.

4.   Wong, H. (1991). The first days of school. Sunnyvale, CA: Harry K. Wong Publications (p. 171-2).

5.   Wong, H. (1991). The first days of school. Sunnyvale, CA: Harry K. Wong Publications (p. 94).

6.   Kronowitz, E. L. (2008). *The teacher's guide to success*. Boston: Pearson Education (p. 185).

7.   Dreikurs, Rudolf retrieved from http://en.wikipedia. org/wiki/Rudolf_ Dreikurs.

8.   11 Techniques for better classroom discipline. Adapted from an article called: "A Primer on Classroom Discipline: Principles Old and New" by Thomas R. McDaniel, *Phi Delta Kappan*, September 1986. Retrieved from http://www.honorlevel.com/techniques.xml.

9.   Wong, H. (1991). *The first days of school*. Sunnyvale, CA: Harry K. Wong Publications (p. 171-2).

10. Gordon, T. (1977). *Teacher effectiveness training*. New York: David McKay.

11. Assertive discipline retrieved from www.derby.ac.uk/ telmie/private/ plymouth/socemassdisc.htm.

EDUCATIONAL LEGALESE 101

In our years of working with preservice teachers, we continue to be amazed at the enthusiasm and interest generated when students engage in discussions of school law and school finance. The knowledge students take away is empowering and instructive. This is what making meaning is all about. We call these two chapters the "cocktail party units." We call them "cocktail party units" because we are not trying to create students who are attorneys or accountants; we are simply trying to share enough to be intellectually instructive at a gathering when the discussion moves to school law or school finance. The gathering might be at the local library, the softball field, the school lounge, the kiosk at the airport, the local coffee shop, a bench in the park, or yes, even a cocktail party. We enjoy watching preservice teachers learn what "inside and outside millage" refers to, and finding the answer to "can I search a student?" These two chapters are meant to provide a general knowledgebase base of the role of law and finance in what we do everyday.

Many say we live in a litigious society, but luckily most novice and veteran teachers do not have many occasions to find themselves involved in litigation. It may appear that a week does not pass without reading or hearing about some teacher or student who steps over the line and ends up in hot water. Those cases are happily few and far between and the majority of level headed hard working educators stay safely above the fray. It is important however, that every teacher, whether new or seasoned, possess a working knowledge of how our legal system is organized, the court cases that have shaped our educational system, and basic teacher and student rights. This chapter will discuss the organization of our legal structure, the federal, state, and local role in education, key legal cases, and the rights of students and teachers.

Goals and Functions of Laws

"Laws are rules and regulations made and enforced by government to regulate the conduct of people within a society."[1] The goals and functions of laws are fairly simple and speak to the care of the collective society. These include the protection of basic human rights, protection of fairness, resolution of conflicts, promotion of order and stability, representation of the will of the majority, and protection of the rights of the minority.[1] Teachers in times past were considered to serve in the role of the parent, or *in loco parentis,* while students were in their care at school. The idea of teachers serving as surrogate parents has declined over the years, but high ethical and moral expectations of teachers remain. In fact, Alexander and Alexander note that when signing a teaching contract, "you accept certain legal rights, professional responsibilities, and ethical obligations that will underscore and guide your behavior."[2] The best advice for novice teachers comes from a professor of educational administration and school law who suggests that before you act, you must stop and ask yourself, "Am I prepared to defend the decisions I have made?"[3] Carefully ponder what headline your behavior will generate if printed on the front page of the community newspaper. Food for thought!

Organization of our Legal System

Our legal system is comprised of courts at the local, state, and federal levels. Cases involving education are heard in either state or federal court, and typically initiate in the state municipal or superior court. If the plaintiff, or the person who is suing, is not satisfied with the ruling in the municipal or superior court, they may seek a ruling from the state appellate court, and then from the state supreme court. The purpose of the appellate court is to hear appeals from municipal and county courts. A plaintiff or litigant who *still* is not satisfied with the state court decision, may request to move to the federal court system, which includes district courts, circuit courts and the Supreme Court.

The power vested in the federal court system comes from the United States Constitution and all three courts serve a distinct purpose. There are 94 judicial districts in the U.S. and its territories, with at least one district court in each state. The district court is the trial court of the federal court system. The 94 districts are organized into 12 circuits, and each of the 12 circuits has a court of appeals. An appeals court only hears cases from its own territory. And because each territory is different with different laws, the decisions from one circuit to another can look very different. A litigant who has been heard at the state or federal system and is *still* not satisfied, may request that the United States Supreme Court hear the case. At least four of the nine Supreme Court judges must agree to "hear" the case and because each geographic region has its own rulings, the judges may depend heavily on the prior rulings of the circuit court in deciding the case.

Federal, state, and local role in education

Traditionally there has been considerable debate over what role the federal government should play in education. Some feel the United States Department of Education should take a strong lead in establishing and implementing school policy in an effort to ensure educational opportunities for disadvantaged students. Others advocate a more conservative approach, leaving school governance decisions to the state legislature and local school boards. You may remember from eighth grade history that the federal government, as outlined in U.S. Constitution, does not specifically address how to govern schools. Through the Tenth Amendment of the Constitution, school governance is delegated to each of the nearly 14,400 public school districts in the 49 states to educate over 48 million students (the exception is Hawaii who maintains one state run system). The states likewise turn the power of running schools over to each local school district and their local school board.

Waves of Reform Movements

There have been many shifts in the federal government's role in educational policy over the last 50 years. These shifts have come in the form of reform movements. The purpose of educational reform is to improve academic outcomes for the nation's students. These shifts can be described as waves of reform movements. *The Elementary and Secondary Education Act of 1965 (ESEA)* marked the government's initial move to implement policy for public schools. This intervention was a reaction to a growing discrepancy between the achievement of students from higher socioeconomic status and those considered disadvantaged. This act greatly expanded the federal role by providing funds to create programs such as Title I, bilingual education, and free and reduced lunch. These, and other programs, attempted to provide support for poor students in the hopes of increasing their academic achievement. ESEA marked the first nationwide federal policy shift in schools, but it was not the first time the government attempted to address inconsistencies in educational achievement. Researcher Kevin R. Kosar expertly chronicles the history of federal education policy on his *Federal Education Policy History website* at www.scribd.com/Kevinrkosar.

Historically, political attention was drawn to the state of our schools with the Soviet launch of Sputnik in 1957. Another country, not to mention that it was the Soviet Union, sending the first artificial satellite into space moved the United States to believe that our educational superiority was threatened, particularly in science and math.[4] In response, the federal government shifted America's educational priorities by increasing funding to schools, specifically targeting science and math programs. Fearing that America's children were not achieving at levels comparable to other countries, politicians established statewide minimum competency testing during the 1970's. This period of reform focused on teaching and testing basic skills to ensure that each child would achieve at least minimum competency by graduation. In 1983 the nation came face to face with the most pivotal educational document in American history. An excerpt from researcher John Goodlad 's report reads:

If an unfriendly foreign power had attempted to impose on America the mediocre educational performance that exists today, we might well have viewed it as an act of war. As it stands, we have allowed this to happen to ourselves. We have even squandered the gains in student achievement made in the wake of the Sputnik challenge. Moreover, we have dismantled essential support systems, which helped make those gains possible. We have, in effect, been committing an act of unthinking, unilateral educational disarmament. (Excerpt from A Nation at Risk[5])

A Nation at Risk: The Imperative for Educational Reform, [5] an infamous open report to the American people is credited with lighting the proverbial fire under the effort to increase student achievement and accountability. This 1980's reform effort was led by educational researchers such as John Goodlad, who promoted a focus on teaching fewer subjects in more depth. This decade was also marked by affording more control to teachers to redefine schools and focus on teaching fewer subjects.[6] Second-guessing the minimum competency push of the 1970's, educators feared that minimum standards had become maximum expectations. This led to public perception that academic content had been "watered down" especially in the poorer school districts.[7] The release of *A Nation at Risk* drew needed attention to the challenges of adequately serving all students, and once again created a fury of reform initiative discussions. These discussions conveniently placed the blame for the lack of academic success squarely on the bruised shoulders of the public school system.[8]

The decades of the 80's and 90's focused on what can be called the "full-service school".[6] This wave of reform promoted the education of the *total child* educationally and socially by recognizing the need for a network of services to meet the needs of poverty-stricken children. From there, we moved into our current educational period, which at its core, is the quest for educator accountability, curriculum standards, and educational options. You are part of this 21st century standards-based education reform initiative of which the *No Child Left Behind Act of 2001* (NCLB) has taken center-stage. NCLB is a revised or *reauthorized* version of the Elementary and Secondary Education Act of 1965, and focuses on improving the academic achievement of under performing students. Current reform efforts put you, as a new teacher, on the front burner so to speak, in a quest to raise the bar for the academic achievement of a new generation. Until this period in time, America's neighborhood public schools had been the cornerstone of the American public school system, but that would soon change. Chapter seven discusses standards based education and accountability in more detail.

State and Local Control of Schools

As discussed, the 10th Amendment of the Constitution passes the power to govern the schools to the states, which in turn empowers local school districts. This significant and seemingly haphazard system explains why from state to state, city to city, and town to town, every district may have its own rules and regulations. What is permitted in this district is not allowed in another district and what is required in this district is not permitted in that district. While this may add to the confusion from one district to the next, it is also what allows each school district to maintain its own unique and dynamic characteristics.

One district may not consider students absent on the opening day of "hunting season," while another district may assemble their five high schools for an All City Pep Band Celebration. Some districts may offer students a choice of attending a variety of high schools such as art focused schools, single gender environments, college preparatory schools, or S.T.E.M. Schools (Science, Technology, Engineering & Math), while in another district students may be permitted to leave school early to tend to their "show" animals at the local fair. Further, district norms and customs may vary in the holidays observed. For instance, holidays such as Ramadan, Martin Luther King, Jr. Day, Yom Kippur, and Columbus Day are not celebrated in all school districts. Perhaps you can recall activities that uniquely characterize your home school and community.

The State Department of Education and the State Board of Education monitor current laws and regulations and have historically addressed difficult and controversial issues such as desegregation and school finance reform. In recent history the State Department's role has largely centered on developing and implementing state assessment requirements and collecting and reporting student progress.[9] Local control of schools allows districts to represent the culture of their individual communities. All local municipalities, with the power given to them from the state, have school boards. In addition to adhering to state law (Ohio Revise Code), local boards create their own policies that govern their schools. Individuals elected or appointed to the school board are meant to represent the community; that is people just like you and me. School boards are very powerful and generally the state and federal courts do not routinely get entangled in their local decision-making power. All boards maintain similar responsibilities, one of the most important is the hiring and firing of the superintendent. Kaplan and Owing[1] describe the duties of the local school board as:

1. Setting a vision for the district

2. Establishing the standards

3. Assessing student learning outcomes

4. Assigning responsibility for student outcomes

5. Dedicating resources to support the district's goals and objectives

6. Monitoring the organizational climate

7. Establishing trust among stakeholders

8. Seeking ways to continue improvement in the areas mentioned above

The job of a school superintendent, called the chief executive officer (CEO) in some districts, is a challenging and demanding position. The strength, expertise, and leadership of the superintendent are critical and have a great impact on the success of the district. The role and duties of the superintendent can vary from job to job, but all report directly to the board of education and will share common general duties. These common duties include school operations (building and facilities management, rules and regulations, administrative processes, ensuring appropriate funding, and creation of standards for educational achievement); district administration (financial budgets, personnel contracts, records and documentation, and annual reports); staff management (maintenance of appropriate staff, defining roles and responsibilities of staff, staff professional development, staff and student discipline procedures); and board of education liaison (maintaining efficient communication between the board, schools, and community, and providing all board requests).

Key Constitutional Amendments

In addition to the 10th Amendment, there are other Constitutional Amendments that have implications for teachers. Many of the court decisions that have shaped the parameters of teachers and student rights have come from the First, Fourteenth and Fourth Amendments.

The First Amendment protects the rights to freedom of speech, freedom of the press, and freedom of religion. Under the First Amendment are two clauses; the Establishment Clause and the Free Exercise Clause. The Establishment Clause states that the government cannot establish a national religion or show a preference to one religion over another. In the interpretation of the Establishment Clause the courts refer to a three-pronged test from a 1971 court decision (Lemon v. Kurtzman) to answer the following:

❑ Does the act have a non-secular (religious) purpose?

❑ Does the act advance or inhibit religion?

❑ Does the act promote the entanglement of government and religion?

The Free Exercise Clause protects the rights of free speech and expression and is interpreted using a two-pronged test where:

❑ The plaintiffs must show that the government action causes injury to their sincerely held beliefs, and

❑ The government must show that there is a strong public need to restrict the act and that no other less restrictive means are possible.

The Fourteenth Amendment is divided into two clauses. The Due Process Clause protects liberty (reputation, integrity, and honor) and the Equal Protection Clause protects property (something of which you have a vested interest such as job, tenure, and benefits). Kaplan and Owings explain that the 14th Constitutional Amendment addresses student's rights in suspension and expulsion as well as teachers' rights in contracts and termination. When a student is suspended, it is an interruption of their right to an education. In *Goss v. Lopez (1975)* the United States Supreme Court ruled that a suspension of less than ten days of school requires **procedural due process.** The Fourteen Amendment stipulates that a student recommended for suspension must receive oral or written notice of the charges, an explanation of the charges against them, and an opportunity to present their side of the events. Expulsion from school constitutes a long term separation from school and requires more formal procedures.[10]

The Fourth Amendment guarantees "The right to be free from unreasonable government searches and seizures and to be secure in their person, houses, papers, and effects."[11] The Fourth Amendment protects the right to privacy for students from searches that are not warranted or are unreasonable. Unlike the "probable cause" required for police searches, schools need only show a "reasonable cause" to search students. The most pivotal court decision used to guide search and seizure practice was *New Jersey v. TLO (1985)*. This case concerned a teacher who caught two girls smoking in the bathroom. One of the girls admitted to the act, but T.L.O adamantly denied the act. The principal searched T.L.O.'s purse and found cigarettes. In reaching for the cigarettes he also saw rolling papers and decided to empty the contents of the purse. Upon empting the purse the principal found a list of people who reportedly owed her money, a large roll of dollar bills, marijuana, a pipe, and empty plastic bags.[12] After confessing to police that she was selling marijuana at school she was sentenced to probation. T.L.O. appealed the decision claiming that the search was not legal under the Fourth Amendment requirement of probable cause. The United States Supreme Court ruled that after seeing the cigarettes and then the rolling papers, the principal had reasonable suspicion to search T.L.O.'s purse further. In this decision the courts considered (1) whether the search was justified at its inception, and (2) whether the search was reasonably related in scope to the circumstances that justified the interference in the first place.[12] Over time the courts have made rulings that are pivotal in nature with far reaching effects. These seminal cases are referred to as *case law* and are used as a guide for deciding subsequent cases. Below is a collection of seminal case law decisions that are considered as a guide for similar cases.

Seminal Cases in the Rights of Teachers

Freedom of Speech (First Amendment)	Pickering v. Board of Education (1968)	Under the First Amendment, a teacher has the right to comment on issues of public concern
Search and Seizure (Fourth Amendment)	New Jersey v. TLO (1985)	School authorities may search a student if the search is justified and there is reason to believe a wrong doing has been committed
Teacher Contracts (Fourteenth Amendment)	Board of Regents of State Colleges v. Roth (1972)	Entitles teachers to fair and adequate information to protect them from arbitrary and capricious termination

Separation of Church and State (First Amendment)	Lee v. Weisman (1992)	Schools may honor a moment of silence provided it does not have a secular purpose
Impairment & Teacher Dismissal (Fourteenth Amendment)	School Board of Nassau County v. Arline (1987)	Teachers cannot be terminated due to a physical impairment or contagious disease
Union Membership (First Amendment)	Lehnert v. Ferris Faculty Association (1991)	Teachers cannot be mandated to pay union fees other than those for collective bargaining

Seminal Cases in the Rights of Students

Freedom of Speech (First Amendment)	Tinker v. Des Moines Independent Community School District (1969)	Students have a right to Freedom of Speech under the First Amendment as long as it does not disrupt the school process
Freedom of Speech (First Amendment)	Bethel School District v. Fraser (1986)	Schools have the right to discipline students who use inappropriate and/or offensive speech
Freedom of the Press (First Amendment)	Hazelwood School District v. Kuhlmeir (1988)	School sponsored, school funded news papers can be censored by school authorities, but school officials may not censor publications created at the students' expense
Freedom of Access to the Printed Word (First Amendment)	Board of Education, Island Trees Union Free School District No. 26 v. Pico (1982)	School boards may not remove materials from students to stifle ideas based on their personal beliefs
Student Due Process (Fourteenth Amendment)	Goss v. Lopez (1975)	Students are entitled to procedural due process because suspension is an interruption to their right to an education
Sexual Harassment	Franklin v. Gwinnett County Public Schools (1992)	Students who are sexually victimized may sue for monetary damages
Separation of Church and State (First Amendment)	Santa Fe Independent School v. Doe (2000)	Student led prayer violates separation of church and state
School Attendance and Choice	Zelman v. Simmons-Harris (2002)	Students may attend private and religious schools using public vouchers

Corporal Punishment	Ingraham v. Wright (1977)	Schools may introduce corporal punishment if allowed by state law

The seminal cases above represent the basis for substantial litigation. Below is a synopsis of legal terms and concepts that may be of interest to teachers.

Breach of Contract	A failure to provide what was stipulated in an agreement
Child Abuse	Teachers are required to report suspected sexual, physical, or emotional child abuse and neglect to school authorities or social services
Child Benefit Theory	Allows state monies to be used for students attending non public schools for the benefit of the child
Copyright Act	Teachers must obtain publisher permission before using published materials
Duty of Care	A responsibility requiring a standard or reasonable care for acts that could harm others
Fair Use	Allows the limited use of copyrighted materials
Lemon Test	A three pronged test to determine if excessive entanglement exists between church and state
Liability	Negative consequences (monetary rewards) resulting from inadequate performance
Litigants	Parties involved in a law suit
Negligence	Failure to provide the precautionary care that would be reasonable by the average person
Plaintiff	The person who is suing or seeking some sort of relief
Procedural Due Process	Procedures must be followed before a person can be deprived of a right or interest (right to education in the case of suspension)
Reasonable Suspicion	A legal standard that reliable information has been received suggesting that wrongdoing has occurred. A lesser standard than probable cause
Sexual Harassment	Uninvited and unwelcome sexual advances, quid pro quo (something for something), and hostile work environment
Substantive Due Process	Prohibits the government from infringing on fundamental constitutional liberties.
Tenure	A provision that a teacher is afforded a continuing contract and protected from arbitrary termination
Title IX	Prohibits the consideration of gender to grant awards, financial aid, scholarships, financial aid

Tort	Harm that one person causes another for which the courts may award damages (civil wrong)
Zero Tolerance Policy	Regardless of circumstance, the implementation of previously established consequences

Teacher Contracts

Teaching in public schools from kindergarten to twelfth grade requires teachers to have a valid teaching license issued by the state. Most states require a criminal background check and with the increasing popularity of electronic media, more and more employers are using social networking sites as part of their employment screening procedures.[13] With this in mind teaching candidates should be mindful of what is posted on their social network sites. Generally, first year teachers are hired on a probationary status. The state of Ohio issues "limited contracts," which extend from one to five years. If the district decides to **non-renew** the contract after the contract term, the teacher must be notified in writing by April 30.[14a] A teaching contract is a legal agreement between the teacher and the board of education and once a contract is signed the teacher is bound to abide by the employment conditions as established by local and state law. The contract will specify the scope of duties and the annual pay.

After the limited contract term, typically three to five years, teachers may be issued a **continuing contract,** or tenure. A continuing contracts stays in effect until a teacher resigns or retires.[14b] Tenure is a measure of increased job security that ensures that a teacher cannot be fired without adhering to the Fourteenth Amendment's Due Process Clause. Under the Fourteenth Amendment, tenured teachers cannot be dismissed without a formal hearing and the demonstration of sufficient proof to satisfy the legal requirements for removal from the position. The teacher has the opportunity to challenge the evidence.[15] A **supplemental contract** is one that is issued by the board of education for additional duties outside the regular school day, such as club advisor, coaching, or driver's education.

As outline by Ohio school law, a licensed administrator evaluates new teachers twice a year. One evaluation must be completed before January 15 with the teacher receiving a written report by January 25. The second evaluation must be completed between February 10 and April 1 with the teacher receiving a written report by April 10.[14c]

Professional Organizations and Collective Bargaining

A professional organization or union represents most teachers. Professional organizations exist to protect, guide, and set standards for employees. Teacher unions play a significant role in most school districts. The two largest are the National Education Association (NEA) and the American Federation of Teachers (AFT). The NEA is the largest professional organization in the nation and has nearly 3 million members. The AFT, a labor oriented union, has experienced philosophical differences with the NEA in the past, but today they share many of the same philosophies. Both focus on creating professional conditions, negotiating improved salaries, and providing opportunities to join political action committees.

Typically, a building representative will contact new teachers before school begins to explain the importance of the union in a teacher's career. This "sales pitch" will include the yearly dues schedule. Keep in mind that unions serve many great purposes, the most important include setting the conditions of the workplace and contract negotiations.

To Join or Not to Join

When deciding whether to become a member you should consider several factors:

1. Does the local union have a positive or negative history? The easiest way to decide is to talk to other teachers. They will know if the union supports teachers or just collects the dues.

2. Does the contract address the employment conditions? Do you understand the conditions? The most important role the union will play will be with the negotiated agreement with the board of education. If the conditions need altered, only members of the union will have a voice.

3. Does the school practice "Fair Share?" The idea behind "fair share" is relatively simple. Since all teachers benefit from the union contract, regardless of union membership, each should pay equivalent "dues." Many states have the right to receive dues regardless of the teachers desire to join. If a teacher chooses not to join, the dues may be used for a charity or political action committee.

4. Has the union been part of a strike lately? Or, better yet, is a strike imminent? When a teacher accepts a teaching position, it is important to be aware of the financial outlook of the district. Strikes are never pretty and often leave long-lasting feelings of negativity. If a strike is possible, it may not be the best time to join the union. However, be aware that if a strike occurs, crossing the picket line against the teaching staff may injure relationships, perhaps irrevocably.

At the same time, union membership does not equal job security. If a financial crisis occurs, new teachers are the first to go, and the bad news is, the union is powerless to save new teacher positions. Unfortunately, job security in this business comes from seniority and nothing else. Union funds will be used for professional development opportunities as well as to support personnel to assist in the contract negotiation process. These negotiation experts are irreplaceable and necessary. Whether to join the union or not is a pivotal decision. With membership, comes a voice in the decision-making process, an opportunity to become involved in the political process, and the comfort of knowing there are advocates to speak on the behalf of teachers.

The most important duty of the union is to collectively bargain, or come to an agreement on the scope of duties and work conditions. Some matters in collective bargaining between the teachers' union and the school district are mandatory and others are of interest to a particular district. Some items that may be subject to the bargaining unit negotiations include:[16]

❑ Academic Freedom

❑ Curriculum

❑ Wages and salaries

❑ Benefits

❑ Training

❑ Hours, workload, and teaching responsibilities

❑ Reclassification and reduction

❑ Tenure

❑ Evaluation

❑ Personnel files

❑ Student discipline

❑ Sick leave

In the state of Ohio, the State Employment Relations Board (SERB) guides negotiations in the collective bargaining process. The state enables SERB to oversee the general procedures in the collective bargaining process. Both sides are expected to bargain in good-faith. **Good-faith bargaining** is the "mutual obligation to meet at reasonable times and places to bargain with the intention of reaching an agreement or to resolve questions that arise under the labor contract.[14d] As one might imagine the negotiation process does not always conclude without conflict. The state of Ohio outlines a progression of legal remedies to help reach an amicable resolution. Simplified explanations of these remedies are outlined below.[16] If one side believes there has been a violation of good-faith bargaining they may file an **Unfair Labor Practice** (ULP). If the ULP cannot be resolved, a legal impasse occurs. When an **impasse** is declared, the parties suspend negotiations and move to **mediation,** where a third and neutral party assists both sides to reach a compromise. If mediation fails they may employ a **fact-finder** who reviews and analyzes facts in an attempt to identify common ground. Neither side is mandated to accept the recommendations of the fact-finder. At last resort, the parties may seek an arbitrator. An **arbitrator** performs the same function as a fact-finder, except the parties are bound to accept and comply with the arbitration findings. If the remedies outlined above are not successful and all required procedures have been followed, teachers in Ohio have the right to strike if they provide the mandatory ten-day written notice. A **strike** is defined as the "continuous concerted action in failing report to duty……for the purpose of inducing, influencing, or coercing a change in wages, hours, terms, and other conditions of employment."[14e] You may note that collective bargaining is highly prescribed and complicated; the Ohio Revised Code (RC § 4117.01) provides a detailed description of the process for your information.

As a novice teacher it is impossible to be aware of all the laws pertaining to students, teachers, and the art of teaching. Dr. Patrick Pauken, a Professor of Educational Leadership and School Law has been providing valuable guidance to novice teachers for nearly 15 years. Below he offers his *Top Ten Legal Tips for Educators*;[12] a common sense guide to assist in making appropriate choices and wise decisions in your new teaching position.

Top Ten Legal Tips for Educators

10. Get a copy of the student handbook/code of conduct from the school or school district—AND READ IT!

9. Get a copy of the student handbook/code of conduct from the school or school district—AND READ IT!

8. Keep yourself to the same high standard of care and conduct that you expect from your supervisors, colleagues, and students.

7. Check for liability insurance coverage from the school district.

6. When acting under direction or authority, undertake only those tasks that rest properly within the scope of the employment.

5. When you have authority to delegate tasks and/or decision-making to colleagues and students, do so clearly—with clear direction and clear supervision.

4. If possible, never be alone with only one student---regardless of gender.

3. Respect and balance the rights of ALL interested parties: administrators, board members, teachers, staff, parents, community members, *and yourself*, but especially the *children*.

2. Act reasonable under the circumstances.

1. Good Luck, Have Fun, and Remember the ultimate goal: Education of Children.

Chapter Exercises

1. Research a *Seminal Case* that appears in the Rights of Students section and discuss how the ruling in the case has shaped how schools currently function.

2. Obtain a School Handbook/Code of Conduct from a school district or online and identify the policies that may impact your practice the as a new teacher.

3. Discuss the ways your personal beliefs may conflict with those espoused by the school. What is the best way deal with any conflicts?

4. Identify an educational reform movement and describe the instructional strategies and student outcomes that may have been present.

5. Should teachers be held to a higher ethical standard than other professionals?

   Discuss why or why not.

6. Examine the Facebook page of a class peer. Are there content that a school district might find questionable or distasteful?

Chapter Summary

1. The goals of laws include maintaining a safe and orderly environment and ensuring fairness for all of society.

2. The United States Constitution makes no provisions for the governance of schools, but empowers the states to govern through the Tenth Amendment to the Constitution.

3. There have been several waves of educational reform over the last 60 years. They can be characterized as:

   a. 1957-The launch of Sputnik increased attention to math and science in school.

   b. 1965-The Elementary and Secondary Education Act (ESEA) created programs for students considered disadvantaged.

   c. 1970's-Minimum competency standards and testing assured that each child would achieve minimum standards

   d. 1983-The release of *A Nation at Risk* focused attention on educational researchers who recommended fewer subjects in more depth.

   e. 1990's-Promoted attention to the social and educational needs of students.

    f.   2001-The enactment of No Child Left Behind; an extension or reauthorization of ESEA that focused on measurement of achievement and accountability.

4.   Be prepared to defend the decisions you make and act reasonably under the circumstances.

5.   Get a copy of the student handbook/code of conduct from the school or school district—AND READ IT!

6.   Teachers are held to a higher standard of ethical behavior than people in other professions.

7.   Both students and teachers enjoy rights and responsibilities under the law.

8.   Teachers in Ohio are subject to professional organizations that collectively bargain scope of duties, work conditions, and benefits.

Notes

1.   P. Pauken (Personal Communication September 2009 – Fall 2011). Bowling Green State University.

Alexander, D. & Alexander, K. (2005). American public school law as cited in L. S. Kaplan & W. A. Owings (2011) *American Education: Building a common foundation*. Belmont, CA: Wadsworth (pp. 231).

3.   Pauken, P. D. (2012, in press). Are you prepared to defend the decisions you've made? Reflective equilibrium, situational appreciation, and the legal and moral decisions of school leaders. *Journal of School Leadership, 22*(2).

4.   Kaplan, L. S. & Owings, W. A. (2011). *American Education: Building a common foundation.* Belmont, CA: Wadsworth (p.282).

5.   U. S. Department of Education. (2008). *A Nation at Risk: The Imperative for Educational Reform.* Retrieved from http://www.ed.gov/pubs/ NatAtRisk/ risk.html on July 17, 2008.

6.   Sadker, M. P. & Sadker, D. M. (2005). *Teachers, schools, and society.*(7th ed.) Boston: McGraw Hill (244).

7.   Amrein, A. L. & Berliner, D.C. (2002, March 28). High-stakes testing, uncertainty, and student learning. *Education Policy Analysis Archives, 10*(18). Retrieved April 28, 2003 from http://epaa.asu.edu/epaa/v10n18/.

8.   May, J. J. (2005). Braving the new world of No Child Left Behind. In C. Fulmer & Debowski (Eds.). *Crediting the past, challenging the present, and changing the future.* (pp. 121-131). Lanham, MD: Rowan Littlefield Education.

9.   As cited in Ornstein, A. C., Levine, D. U., & Gutek, G. L. (2011). *Foundations of education*, Belmont, CA: Wadsworth, Cengage Learning (p. 226).

10.   Kaplan & Owings, 2011, (p. 255-256).

11.   Maclin, T. (1993). The central meaning of the Fourth Amendment. *William and Mary Law Review*, 35(1/7), p. 197-249. Retrieved from http://scholarship. law.wm.edu/wmlr.

12.   Ornstein, A. C., Levine, D. U., & Gutek, G. L. (2011). *Foundations of education*, Belmont, CA: Wadsworth, Cengage Learning, (p. 284-285).

13.   Fishman, N. (2011, April 27). *Screening background checks on applicants using Facebook.* Retrieved from http://www.employeescreen.com/iqblog/ background-checks-on-applicants-using-facebook/.

14.   Carey, K. H. (2011) Anderson's Ohio School Law Manual. Matthew Bender & Company/Lexus Nexus.

    a.   p. 633

    b.   p. 633

    c.   p. 818

    d.   p. 216

    e.   p. 255

15.   Alexander, K. & Alexander, M. D. (2001) *American public school law* (5th ed.). Belmont, CA: Wadsworth/Thompson Learning, (p. 671).

16.   Everyday Law Encyclopedia. (nd).*Teacher's Unions/Collective Bargaining.* Retrieved from www.enotes.com/everyday-law-encyclopedia/teacher-s-unions- collective-bargaining/.

School Funding: A Conundrum

In 1991, 15-year old Nathan DeRolph was a student at Sheridan High School in Thornville, Ohio. The schools in Thornville were in disrepair; there were often more students than seats, his biology book was written the year he was born, and at the elementary school, built circa 1913, the attic floor gave way from the weight of the bat feces that had collected on the floor. [1]

The condition of schools such as Nathan's provided the backdrop for the 1991 lawsuit filed in Perry County, Ohio by the Ohio Coalition for Equity and Adequacy of School Funding. The suit was brought on behalf of Nathan DeRolph and *all* the students in Ohio attending schools like those in Thornville. *DeRolph v. State of Ohio* alleged that because school districts depend on property taxes for financial support, students living in areas with higher property values generated more money and therefore had access to more educational opportunities.

To understand how the Ohio funding model works and the impact of DeRolph, consider the following scenario:

Mary is in seventh grade and lives in Workinghard, Ohio where the average price of a home is $100,000 and the average household income is $50,000 per year. Sammy is also in the seventh grade and lives in Upscale, Ohio where the average price of a home is $300,000 and the average household income is $150,000.

Schools generate money from property taxes using the assessed valuation or taxable value of the home. The **assessed value** is 35% of the home's true market value. The true **market value** is the price someone would pay if purchasing the home from the current owners.

Mary's assessed taxable value on her $100,000 home is $35,000 ($100,000 x .35). Sammy's assessed taxable value on his $300,000 home is $105,000 ($300,000 x .35). A mill is the unit of value used to generate funds from taxable property.

A mill is one-tenth (1/10th) of a penny.

❑ For every $100 of assessed value a mill generates .10 (100 x .001).

❑ For every $1000 of assessed value a mill generates $1.00 (1,000 x .001).

❑ For every $100,000 of assessed value a mill generates $100.00 (100,000 x .001).

❑ For every $1,000,000 of assessed value a mill generates $1,000.00 (1,000,000 x .001).

For Mary's home in Workinghard one mill raises $35 ($35,000 x .001). For Sammy's house in Upscale one mill raises $105 ($105,000 x .001). If you haven't guessed yet......it's just a decimal game! Both Workinghard and Upscale each have 3,000 students. Each district needs to raise $200 per student for textbooks and materials this school year for a total of $600,000 for the school year. For the residents of Upsale to raise about $600,000 real dollars, they will need roughly *5,700 mills* (5,700 x $105 = $598,500). For the residents of Workinghard to raise $600,000 real dollars, they will need roughly *17,000 mills* (17,000 mills x $35 = $595,000).

To purchase books and materials the residents of Workinghard will need to pay *3 times* the number of mills than those needed from each resident in Upscale. With an average salary of $50,000 the residents of Workinghard will pay 1.4% of their annual salary on property taxes. The residents of Upscale will pay .7% of their annual salary on property taxes. The residents of Workinghard will pay *two times the percentage of their annual salary* than the residents of Upscale.

If the residents of both communities are raising the exact same amount of money, the residents with the lower annual income actually pay a larger percentage of their income to support their schools. In another example let's suppose each district is asking homeowners to pay 20 mills per year to cover other school costs. The Workinghard homeowner will pay $700 ($35 x 20) in property taxes per year and the homeowner in Upscale will pay $2, 100 ($105 x 20) in property taxes per year. Again, the residents of Upscale raise over 30% (or 3 times) more money with 1 mill than do the residents of Workinghard. The Workinghard residents will have to pay 3 mills for every 1 mill payed in Upscale to raise the same amount of money.

A visual representation of the scenario appears below.

District	Home Market Value	Home Assessed Value	20 Mills Taxes	Annual Income	Percentage of Annual Income for Taxes
Workinghard Local	100,000	35,000	700.00	50,000	1.4
Upscale Local	300,000	105,000	2100.00	300,000	.7

The examples presented are perhaps overly simplistic explanations, but capture the nature of how funding schools with property taxes is inequitable. The more affluent your neighborhood, the less of your income you have to pay.

The Saga of DeRolph I, II, III, and IV

There have actually been four court decisions in *DeRolph v. State of Ohio*. DeRolph I was filed in 1991 and the plaintiffs, the Ohio Coalition for Equity and Adequacy of School Funding, claimed that by relying heavily on property taxes to fund schools the "state failed to provide an efficient" educational system as required by the Ohio Constitution. They also asserted that "schools in areas with higher property values could more easily meet the needs of and provide more opportunities for their students, while students in poorer areas suffered." [1]

In 1997 the Ohio Supreme Court ruled that the state funding system violated the Ohio Constitution and was unconstitutional under the following[2]:

❑ The School Foundation Program (state aid) failed to provide sufficient funds for an adequate education;

❑ The school funding system placed too much reliance on local property taxes;

❑ The State failed to provide adequate funding for school buildings;

❑ The requirement that school districts borrow money through the spending reserve and emergency school assistance loan programs also violated the requirements that the State provide for adequate funding.[3]

The Supreme Court ordered a "complete, systematic overhaul" of the system to be carried out in one year and mandated that the *trial* court follow up to decide if the order for the systematic overhaul was satisfied.[2] The state (General Assembly) did make modifications to the funding system, but they did *not* address the over reliance on property tax. In DeRolph II (May 2000), the Ohio Supreme Court recognized that the state had made changes, but was not satisfied and gave the State another year to fix the funding problem.[2] The third DeRolph decision occurred in September 2001 when the Ohio Supreme Court *retracted* the mandate for a "complete and systematic overhaul."[2] Instead the Court mandated changes to the formula used to decide how state monies were distributed to districts. In turn, the State objected to the Supreme Courts' mandated changes citing the exorbitant costs associated with such mandates. The Supreme Court acquiesced and ordered both the General Assembly and the Ohio Coalition to engage in negotiations with a professional mediator to find an acceptable remedy. In December 2002, the mediation failed and the Ohio Supreme Court upheld the DeRolph III decision noting that the *Ohio General Assembly had failed to meet the mandates of DeRolph I and II and that the school funding was still unconstitutional.*[3]

The DeRolph decisions have obviously become seminal case law, but Ohio is not the only state to garner such honors. Other states have brought cases challenging public school fiscal inequities. In *Serrano v. Priest (1971)*, for instance, the California Supreme Court ruled that the "quality of a child's education should not be dependent on the wealth of his parents and neighbors."   And in a 1973 Texas case, the United States Supreme Court over turned a lower court decision ruling that funding inequities did not violate the Constitution (*San Antonio Independent School District v. Rodriguez*).[4]

Property Valuation

In addition to property tax, districts may also vote an income tax or a sales tax or any combination of the three to generate funds for their schools. In 2011 nearly 30% of the districts in Ohio had a school income tax on the ballot.[5] Many states and some communities rely on income tax and sales tax support, though they are not widely used as the major portion of local school funding. The majority of school funds are raised locally from taxes levied on real property and tangible personal property. *Real property* refers to the buildings and grounds held by individuals and businesses. Real property is divided in two groups: Group 1 is residential and agricultural property and Group 2 is commercial and industrial property.[3] *Tangible property* tax is paid on business machinery, equipment, and inventory. Taxes on utilities such as power plants and phone companies is called public utility tangible personal property.[3] The *total valuation* of the district refers to the total value of the district; including buildings, businesses, and land. Property taxes are the most widely used method to raise revenue at the local level.

Inside, Outside, Effective Mills and Phantom Revenue

The majority, or about 50% of school funding comes from local property taxes. Approximately 44% comes from state foundation aid and 6% comes from the federal government.[5] As explained, local funds for schools come from property taxes raised through a unit of value called a mill. Citizens vote on the majority of the mills levied. In addition to the voted mills, the State Constitution allows 1% of assessed property value to be collected *without* a vote. These unvoted mills are called *inside mills.* Inside mills account for a small amount of revenue. *Outside or voted mills* account for the balance of the local school funds. Voted mills are raised through tax levies.[6]

"The Ohio Constitution prohibits districts from collecting taxes on the growth in property value."[7] In other words, when the market or the real value of the home increases, the school district cannot capitalize on the increased value. In fact the homeowner's taxes are adjusted or reduced to ensure no tax increase. *Effective mills* represent the difference between the original voted taxes raised and taxes that *would have been generated* at the property's increased value. This *tax reduction factor* is also known as the *House Bill 920 factor (HB 920).* HB 920 was enacted in 1976 and affects the outside mills only.[3]

The difference between the voted rate and the reduction rate is often referred to as *Phantom Revenue.*[3] The term phantom revenue is used because the increased property tax value the schools *do not* receive because of HB 920 is what the state uses to figure the state funding (state foundation aid) to the district.[6] Each year school districts receive an amount of money for each child in the district (per pupil state foundation aid). The money the local district receives from the state is based, in part, on the funds generated from local property taxes. In other words, the state may figure the districts' per pupil state aid funds based on the *current* market value of the districts' property, when in fact, the district may not be receiving the benefit of the increased property value, hence the term phantom revenue. This would be like your boss giving you a big raise *on paper*, not in real dollars; *but* turning in the paper amount to the Internal Revenue Service (IRS) so you pay federal taxes on income you *did not* receive. The difference between what your paycheck *actually is* and what your boss reports to the IRS with your big fat raise is phantom revenue. It is on paper, but you are not actually receiving it. As you can imagine, this is a real sore spot for school districts.

Homestead Rollback

Under state law each homeowner receives a 10% tax discount or reduction to lighten their tax burden. If it is an owner occupied residence (as opposed to rental property) an additional 2.5% is added for a total of reduction of 12.5%. The state in turn reimburses the school district for the 10% or 12.5% discount as a part of the state foundation aid.[3]

Tax Levies

Tax levies are the means by which the millage dollars are collected. School districts are *dependent* on communities to approve the levies placed on the ballot and the district must indicate the purpose of the tax levy. The 3 tax levies most widely used include: Operating Levies, Permanent Improvement Levies, and Bond Levies.

Property taxes raised through **Operating Levies** may be used for any legal expenditure voted by the board of education. These may include expenditures such as teacher salaries, utility payments, and recreational activities, and are typically identified for the day-to-day expenses associated with operating the schools. **Permanent Improvement or PI Levies** may not be used for district day-to-day expenses and are to be used for long lasting improvements such as building maintenance, bus purchases, or other educational equipment. **Bond Issues** are targeted for major renovations or new buildings. Levies can be voted for a **limited** amount of time, one to five years, or they can be voted as **continuing**. A continuing levy is voted indefinitely or until it is revoked by the voters or if the district decides not to collect the tax.[5]

There are several types of levies:

Emergency Levy is a tax that fulfils a specific purpose with a maximum of 5 years. An emergency levy can be renewed.

Dollar or Millage Incremental Levy is a tax that is also known as a phase-in levy. Taxes can be raised by increasing or decreasing the millage rate or the dollar amount over a period of 10 years. For instance, the first 3 years might be 2 mills, the next 3 years might add 1 or more mills, and so on. A dollar incremental may seek to raise 1 million dollars over 5 years on an incremental basis.

Renewal Levy is a tax that is intended to renew a limited levy when it expires. The renewal levy must be identified for the same purpose as the original levy at the same millage rate.

Replacement Levy is a levy much like a renewal, except it replaces the previous levy, but is levied at the original millage rate and not the effective rate. This allows the district to benefit from an increase in property values.[6]

Changes in State Funding Models

As mentioned earlier in the chapter, school districts receive about 44% of their funding from the state based on a formula. The base formula had remained relatively unchanged from the 1970's to 2009. The model was based on allotting funds to school districts on a per pupil model through the Ohio School Foundation Program. In 2010 the current governor of Ohio introduced an Evidence-Based Model (EBM). The EBM was created to eliminate the phantom revenue created by the difference between increased property values and the tax reduction factor. The latest governor however proposes to eliminate the EBM in favor of a new formula for funding schools. Until the "new" formula is established, a "Bridge" formula, based again on a per pupil calculation, will be used.

Historically, there have been a myriad of concerns with the model used to fund Ohio's schools. In 2011 over 6.5 billion in state aid dollars were provided for the 614 city, local, and exempted village districts, 49 joint vocational schools, 300 community schools and one STEM school. Of the 6.5 billion, $271 million was transferred to charter or community schools and 79 million was transferred to private schools. [6]

Persistent state foundation funding issues:

❑ Lack of adequate funding for students identified with special needs;

❑ Lack of adequate funding for districts with high poverty rates;

❑ Persistent inequities between poor and affluent districts;

❑ Lack of adjustment for educational costs of schools in different geographic areas;

❑ Lack of correlation to effective strategies;

❑ HB 920; and

❑ Passage of less than 50% of the state's tax levies in the last 5 years.[6]

The Ohio Constitution requires the General Assembly to provide and fund "a thorough and efficient system of common schools throughout the State."

Ohio's funding model is based on a theory of shared responsibility,[5] but there continues to be considerable debate as to what the system should look like. It is fortunate that most teachers find that the funding debate is not one that impacts the joy of their day-to-day teaching experience.

Chapter Activities

1. On the Ohio Department of Taxation website find the Tax Data Series link and look up the worksheet that contains:

    School District Data, Property Tax Data by School District, Taxable Property Values, Taxes Levied, Tax Rates for Current Expenses, and Average Property Values Per Pupil

    On the worksheet locate your home school district, or a school district of choice and report on the following:

    a.   Total Value of the District

    b.   The total millage voted in the community (Real & Tangible)

    c.   The rank out of 614 districts

    d.   The Average Amount Spent Per Pupil

    Given the information, what inferences can you make about the district? What are the differences between your district and the district's of your class peers?

2. Research the most recent tax levies in your home district. Describe the type of levies the school district put on the ballot. How many mills were requested? Did the voters pass them? For what period of time?

3. Brainstorm solutions to Ohio's funding model. Do you think they discussed these in the DeRolph decisions? Why or why not? What do you think the state should do?

4. Research the funding models for California and Michigan. How does California's model differ from Ohio's? How can Michigan's recent school funding history be used to inform Ohio's continued funding dilemma? What types of funding models are in Hawaii, New Mexico, Washington, and West Virginia?

Chapter Summary

1. Funding for schools is largely raised through property taxes, but sales and income tax may be used as well.

2. The 1991 DeRolph case challenged the use of property taxes to fund schools claiming that resources for schools should not be dependent upon the wealth of the community. The Ohio Supreme Court ruled that Ohio's over reliance on property taxes violated Ohio's Constitution by "failing to provide for a thorough and efficient system of common schools."

3. Property taxes for schools are based on the assessed value of the home and as the value of the home increases, school districts do not collect additional tax dollars unless another levy is voted at the new assessed value rate.

4. A mill is equal to one-tenth of a penny. For every $1000.00 of assessed value a mill generates $1.00. Property taxes are raised through levies. Money raised through operating levies can be used for any legal expenditure by the board; permanent improvement funds can be used for long lasting improvements; and bond issues are for buildings. Levies can be voted as limited or continuing; replacement or renewal; and for a set or incremental dollar or millage amount.

Notes

1. Ohio History Central. (n. d.) *DeRolph v. State of Ohio.* Retrieved from www. ohiohistorycentral.org/entry.php?rec=2055.

2. Ohio Legislative Black Caucus: Policies & Issues. (n.d.). DeRolph history and Background.

   Retrieved from http://olbcfoundation.org/pdf/Derolph%20History%20 and%20Background.pdf.

3. Pausch, F., Bristol, R., Economus, J., Driscoll, W. P., Fleeter, H. B. & Levin, R. A. (2003). *Making sense out of school finance.* Columbus, Ohio: Ohio School Boards Association, (p.1).

4. Parkay, F.W. & Stanford, B.H. (2004). *Becoming a teacher*, (6th ed.). Boston, MA: Pearson Allyn and Bacon (p. 182).

5. Department of Education. (2011). *Department of Taxation.* Retrieved from http://tax.ohio.gov/divisions/school_district_income/index.stm.

6. Ohio Department of Education. (2011). *State funding for schools.* Retrieved from http://www.education.ohio.gov/GD/Templates/Pages/ODE/ODEDetail. aspx?page=3&TopicRelationID=990&ContentID=112242.

7. Ohio's Current School Funding System. (n.d.). *School Funding Matters.* Retrieved from www.schoolfundingmatters.org/content/FundingToday. aspx (p.3).

ACCOUNTABILITY IS THE NAME OF THE GAME

Jennifer Erin is a secondary Language Arts teacher for Cleveland Metropolitan Schools, Cleveland, Ohio

While I was student teaching in an eleventh grade Language Arts class, I remember my cooperating teacher informing me of the importance of the Ohio Graduation Test (OGT). I didn't flinch. After all, I was already aware of achievement tests, valued added, district report cards and the dreaded 'teaching to the test.' Now in my first teaching position and desperate to establish my credibility, I was anxious to become part of the solution. I decided to ambitiously accept an opportunity to provide intense and individualized instruction after school to students taking the OGT.

And I was prepared, or so I thought.

I collected online practice OGT testing materials, vocabulary and reading strategies, and reading and writing exercises appropriate for individual or group work. My ambition did little to abate my lack of preparation, however. Had I taken the time to research the students who qualified for OGT assistance, I would have learned that the majority of the students were "at-risk" poor readers, poor writers and needed intense instruction far beyond the basics. Now I was scared.

Students reading at a fifth grade level have a hard time comprehending the test material; therefore they cannot analyze, cannot synthesize, and cannot apply the information necessary to pass this huge test. And, all components of the OGT require reading for completion.

So, where was I supposed to go from there? What was I supposed to do? I didn't know how to teach students to read. I didn't know how to teach a student the basics not acquired in elementary school. I could not teach comprehension strategies to students

who did not have the prior knowledge to make new strategies effective or applicable. What did Harry Wong say to do in such a situation? What about Gardner, Brofenbrenner, Gesell, Maslow, and Piaget? What did they say to do?

There were no quick answers or quick fixes. While my college coursework and experiences in the classroom were great for my average everyday students, I had no specific tools to address the problem. With my ambition balloon a bit deflated, I relied on my colleagues, peers and the students to help me realize what to do -- how to teach. It was more work than I ever imagined, and I learned so much. Mostly I learned that students who were poor readers did not have any less ambition to be successful than their academically astute peers. I learned they were great kids that no one really knew. I learned I had been wrong about a great deal in my short life. And I learned that I had the tools all along to do the job. I learned that I was a teacher.

Unless you have been living on another planet, or have avoided conversations with breathing educators for the last few years, you have, at a minimum, heard of the No Child Left Behind Act of 2001 (NCLB). So you may ask, what's the big deal? Well the deal is big indeed. Today's teachers (that's you), more than ever in our educational history, have been unwittingly swept up in a national movement toward increased accountability. This accountability movement engages the educational community to establish rigorous academic standards and to define *exactly who is responsible for what* in the student achievement life cycle. The No Child Left Behind Act of 2001, signed into law by President George W. Bush on January 8, 2002, shifted the power to develop school policy from the local level to the federal level. This interruption of local policy control marks a significant change in power in American public schools. This chapter discusses the accountability measures associated with the No Child Left Behind Act of 2001, issues relative to standards-based education, and your role as an educator.

THE ERA OF STANDARDS AND ACCOUNTABILITY

NCLB is a *reauthorization* of the Elementary and Secondary Education Act (ESEA) first passed in 1965. Billed as President Lyndon Johnson's Civil Rights Era "War on Poverty," ESEA, the most sweeping federal legislation in the history of American public schools, emphasized equal access to education and high standards and accountability. [1] ESEA provided the Department of Education distributes funds for the following:

- ❑ Title I: Financial Assistance to Local Educational Agencies (LEA's) for the Education of Children of Low-Income Families;

- ❑ Title II: School Library Resources, Textbooks and Instructional Materials;

- ❑ Title III: Supplementary Educational Centers and Services;

- ❑ Title IV: Educational Research and Training;

- ❑ Title V: Grants to Strengthen State Departments of Education; and

- ❑ Title VI: General Provisions. [2]

The 1965 Act was initially enacted for five years, but has since been reauthorized every five years. [3] The goal of NCLB is to build on the landmark ESEA to ensure that every child achieves proficiency on state-defined educational standards by the end of the 2013-14 school year.[4]

There continues to be a firestorm of debate relative to the implementation of NCLB and its effect on rural, suburban, and urban school districts. Concerns emanate from teachers, administrators, civic groups, legislators, parents, and community stakeholders. Even with the apprehension surrounding NCLB, the good news for teachers is that according to the latest Phi Delta Kappa Gallop Poll of the Public's Attitudes Toward Public Schools, over 70% of Americans say they have trust and confidence in public school teachers. And encouragingly the poll reports that three out of four Americans say they would encourage the brightest person they know to become a teacher. [5]

The original provisions of NCLB require that all districts and schools receiving Title I funds (over half of the nation's public schools) meet the states' definition of "adequate yearly progress" (AYP) goals for all students. AYP, as explained in the next section, refers to the criteria established for the expected academic growth of each student annually. If one student group (as described on page 107 and 108) does not adequately achieve, then the school is not considered to be achieving and receives a "failing" grade. [6] Title I funds are the largest monetary federal investment in education and are targeted for programs designed to improve the academic achievement of students from low-income environments. Schools receiving Title I funds must have at least 40% of the student population from low-income homes, often measured by the number of students receiving free and reduced-price lunch.[7] Schools receiving federal Title I funding who fail to meet AYP for two consecutive years or more, are designated as "in need of improvement" and face increasingly strong consequences.

No Child Left Behind School Improvement Stages

Year 1 of School Improvement*	Must notify parents that the school did not achieve AYP and make them aware that their child can exercise their *school choice* option to attend a higher achieving school.
Year 2 of School Improvement	In addition to school choice, districts must offer supplemental services such as tutoring.
Year 3 of School Improvement	In addition to school choice and supplemental services the school must take corrective action such as replacing staff members or implementing alternative curricula.
Year 4 of School Improvement	In addition to all of the above, schools must engage in restructuring such as replacing all staff, contracting with a private management organization, reopening as a charter school; or some other major restructuring initiative. The planning must take 1 year and the restructuring implementation the next year.

* Actually the third year of NCLB. Schools could not be subject to School Improvement until the 2003-2004 school year.

Like most federal edicts, the No Child Left Behind Act is a very involved and complicated document, one you would have to digest with a dictionary in one hand and headache reliever in the other! So, for the purposes of this handy little book, we have developed a user-friendly synopsis to assist you in understanding the original components of NCLB.

Major Components of the No Child Left Behind Act of 2001

The law mandates that each state is required to establish challenging standards and measures of accountability. Building on the ESEA, NCLB more specifically targets Title funds in the following categories:

- ❑ Title I: Improving the Academic Achievement of the Disadvantaged;
- ❑ Title II: Preparing, Training, and Recruiting High Quality Teachers and Principals;
- ❑ Title III: Language Instruction for Limited English Proficient and Immigrant Students;
- ❑ Title IV: 21st Century schools-Safe & Drug-Free Schools and Communities, 21st Century Community Learning Centers;
- ❑ Title V: Promoting Informed Parental Choice and Innovative Programs; and
- ❑ Title VI: Flexibility and Accountability. [8]

In full compliance of NCLB, the state of Ohio utilizes four major performance measures: state indicators, performance index scores, adequate yearly progress, and value added measures.

- ❑ **State Indicators:**

  - • To meet assessment (Ohio Achievement Assessment) indicators for grades 3 – 8 at least 75% of the students must score 75% or higher on annual tests (one point awarded for each subject passed at each grade level).

  - • To earn the Ohio Graduation Test indicator, at least 85% of the 11th graders must pass the test.

  - • To earn the attendance rate indicator, schools must have an attendance rate of at least 93%.

  - • To earn the graduation rate indicator, schools must have a graduation rate of at least 90%.

- ❑ **Performance Index Score**: This score is a weighted average of achievement of every assessed student (Grades 3 – 8, OGT) with a possible scaled score of 120.

  - • Untested students earn 0 points;
  - • Limited score earns .3 points;

- Basic score earns .6 points;

- Proficient score earns 1.0 points;

- Accelerated score earns 1.1 points; and

- Advance score earns 1.2 points.

❏ **Adequate Yearly Progress:** To achieve AYP, each district must:

- meet goals in math and reading proficiency

- meet attendance rate goals

- meet graduation rate goals

- ensure all 10 subgroups in the district participate in all three criteria above.

❏ AYP is not achieved if any subgroup fails to achieve. Consequences apply for schools not making AYP for two or more consecutive years (School moves to School Improvement Status).

❏ **Value Added Measure:** This score measures the progress students make from one year to the next. Value added affords each district the opportunity to show student growth from year to year even though students may not achieve the 75% passing rate on state assessments.

District accountability measures are published annually in a Local Report Card (LRC) by the Ohio Department of Education. School and district results are compared and ranked locally and nationally. The Local Report Card provides a detailed report on the progress of all four performance measures as well as additional demographic data for each district including:

❏ Student assessment progress in aggregate (total) form and disaggregate form (by student subgroups: Economically disadvantage, Black, non Hispanic, Asian/Pacific Islander, American Indian/Alaskan Native, Multiracial, Hispanic, White, students with Disabilities, Limited English Proficiency, and all students);

❏ Three year tracking of assessment results showing rates of improvement;

❏ Attendance rates;

❏ Graduation rates;

❏ Percentage of school diversity by subgroup including students who are

- Disabled

- Economically disadvantaged and

- Limited English proficient;

❑   Teacher qualifications (Bachelors/Masters);

❑   The school/district designation based on the 4 accountability measures

- Excellent with Distinction;
- Excellent;
- Effective;
- Continuous Improvement;
- Academic Watch; and
- Academic Emergency.

Each school is responsible for "subgroup accountability." *Subgroup accountability* means that schools *must* report annual test results by *each* student group in the school so that achievement may be monitored for progress. These subgroups include race/ethnic groups, students with disabilities, limited English proficient students, and economically disadvantaged students. In an effort to increase student achievement, close achievement gaps, and ensure that a highly qualified teacher teaches every child, every state is required to develop challenging academic standards and assessments. Achievement tests are administered annually to students in grades 3 – 8. The Ohio Graduation Test (OGT) is given to sophomore students, and they may retest as needed before graduation. The resulting test scores are then used to judge if the student, school, and district are making AYP toward becoming proficient in those subjects. To qualify to meet AYP, 95% of *each* student population (subgroup) in the school must participate in annual assessments.

Highly Qualified Teacher

A major purpose of NCLB is to ensure that all students, regardless of race, ethnicity or income have the best teachers possible. Mandating *Highly Qualified Teachers* (HQT) is based on research that points to teacher quality as a major factor in student achievement.[9] This assertion draws little argument since any teacher will proudly acknowledge the major role they play in the instructional success of students. Disagreement does exist, however, in the level of influence teachers *actually* possess in the success of NCLB. Some researchers contend that NCLB fails to consider other variables in the equation that fall far beyond the reach of teachers, such as high mobility rate, high poverty rate, low parent support,[10] lack of community support, and under-resourced schools and facilities.

You have probably spent a minimum of four years in college and now you hear that you must be highly qualified. Well not to worry; you will more than likely graduate as a Highly Qualified Teacher. So what does being highly qualified actually mean? It means that for you to you teach a core subject, you must meet federal and state definition criteria. Core academic subjects include English, language arts, reading, science, mathematics, foreign language, government and civics, history, economics, geography, and the arts (music, visual arts, dance and drama). These guidelines became effective for *all* teachers in 2006. To meet federal guidelines you must have:

1. A minimum of a Bachelor's degree;

2. Full state certification/licensure appropriate to the grade and subject in which you are teaching; and

3. The ability to demonstrate subject area expertise in the core academic subjects you teach in one of the following:

    a   NTE/Praxis-II-State License Exam;

    b. Academic Major or equivalent in Content Area;

    c. Appropriate Master's Degree;

    d. 8-year Professional Certificate;

    e. Permanent Certificate;

    f. National Board Certification; and

    g. Ninety clock hours of appropriate LPDC approvable Professional Development [11]

Each state defines their process for certification/licensure and enjoys the freedom to strengthen requirements as well as create alternate routes to licensure. Additionally, the law requires states consider the variances between elementary and secondary teachers, novice and experience teachers, and small or rural schools where educators often teach multiple subjects.[12] New graduates satisfy the HQT requirements, and the good news is that once you are considered a HQT in a subject and grade level, you will always remain so.

Intervention specialists and HQT

For populations except the most severely disabled, schools teach students who are disabled in inclusionary education settings with their non-disabled peers. The goal of inclusion is to educate all students (both disabled and non-disabled) in common classrooms with instruction from teachers who are experts in their fields (both regular and specialized teachers). This moves from an outdated model of grouping students who are disabled in one classroom (self-contained). Inclusion has changed the role of Special Education teachers, now more appropriately called Intervention Specialists. Because inclusion classrooms have both non-disabled students and students on Individual Education Plans (IEP), intervention specialists who many be "team-teaching" may find they are required to obtain "Highly Qualified Teacher" status in any number of core subjects (English, math, science and social studies). Intervention specialists and veteran teachers must also be highly qualified by the state. No Child Left Behind requires intervention specialists attain:

1.   Bachelor's Degree;

2.   State special education certification or license;

3.   No waiver of licensing requirements (on an emergency, temporary or provisional) and intervention specialists who are teaching "alternative achievement standards" need all the items above. In addition they must:

4.   Meet NCLB requirements of elementary teachers (test of basic skills in multiple core content subjects); or

5.   Meet licensure requirements for secondary level core subject instruction.

Under the Individuals with Disabilities Education Act (2004) school districts are permitted to hire new intervention specialists for a K – 6th grade teaching assignment who demonstrate subject area expertise in the core academic subjects they teach through:

a.   Passage of Praxis II Test in the appropriate area or

b.   Passage of Praxis II Test: Teaching Reading. [12]

Under the Individuals with Disabilities Education Act (2004) school districts are permitted to hire new intervention specialists for a 7 - 12th grade teaching assignment that meet one of the following:

a.   Have an academic major in Language Arts, Science, or Math or

b.   Pass the Praxis II Test: Teaching Reading [12]

New intervention specialists have two years to meet the HQT requirements in the remaining areas of their teaching assignment, as needed. Colleges have begun to offer courses in these areas for intervention specialists. As long as standardized high stakes testing is in place for all student populations, districts will be turning to inclusion and intervention specialists for significant instructional support. Therefore, more and more intervention specialists are finding their roles changing in schools.

High Stakes Testing

As noted, NCLB mandates annual assessments for students. These annual assessments are often referred to as "high stakes testing" because success or failure of the school and/or district is dependent upon this "one-shot" assessment measure. Because success or failure of schools and teachers is based largely on these annual assessment results, the instructional practices of many schools are driven by efforts to comply with NCLB. The demand for higher achievement through more challenging standards and correspondingly more rigorous curriculum, have lead to teacher complaints. Some teachers claim that NCLB influences their instructional and curricular practices because they feel compelled to ignore some aspects of the curriculum, [13] changing instruction from "exploratory, lifelong learning to teaching to the test through drill and kill". [14] Likewise, other teachers argue that the pressure of meeting AYP can cause undue stress on them as well as students.

The truth is, no government or state measure or law should ever derail the *way* you teach your students. "Teaching to the test" may *seem* to be a reality at times, but your day-to-day teaching *does not* have to be compromised.

Teaching to the Test?

We often hear distressed educators lament about "teaching to the test." Please be aware that no curriculum, test, or set of standards should ever prevent you from teaching the way you want to teach. What you are teaching is the established curriculum and the *established curriculum is what is tested*. What reason is there for teaching anything BUT the established curriculum if that is what is to be tested? Would you teach a class to ride a bike and then test them on rowing a boat? My guess is, "No." Testing is the current standardized method of holding educators accountable for student learning. The test content creates the basis for *WHAT* you need to cover. *HOW* you cover the material will *ALWAYS* be up to you and your creativity. Additionally, teachers are encouraged to add their own material, their own personality, and their own style to teaching. Teaching with your own flair and style does not preclude covering the content that is to be tested. There are dozens of ways to teach and assess student learning. Project-based assignments, presentations, research papers, direct instruction, cooperative learning projects, technology tools, multiple intelligence strategies, and Socratic questioning to name a few can be used to cover any and all sorts of topics. If you have a certain type of instruction you enjoy, use it! *There is no reason why curriculum should necessarily dictate the type of instruction.* Likewise, if you enjoy a certain subject in your area, find a way to incorporate that subject into your class setting. It can be done! Use your passion to fuel your instruction. Never let any set of standards guide the way you instruct your students. Do what you do best, and the curriculum will take care of itself.

It is important to develop a timely plan to cover the required material in the allotted time period during the school year. We discussed earlier how planning your first year is a must. Developing a clear-cut plan for each unit will permit you to utilize your own teaching style affording time to relax, knowing all the bases are covered. There is no doubt you will encounter teachers in May in a full-blown panic wondering how they will ever finish the year's curriculum. Those teachers likely failed to plan ahead. So, the first priority when it comes to your curriculum is to SET A PLAN IN PLACE!

NCLB and IDEA

Perhaps one of the most widely debated issues under NCLB is the accountability measure that requires students with disabilities to participate in annual assessments just as their typical peers. Students with disabilities are educated under the Individuals with Disabilities Education Act of 1997 (IDEA), and have been traditionally *individually* accountable to the Individual Education Plan (IEP) with compliance to procedural safeguards. The measures in NCLB represent a major shift from a system based on an individualized accountability model to our current one requiring public accountability.[15]

Districts may develop alternative assessments for students with disabilities, but the standards themselves cannot be changed. This means that the actual tests may be less rigorous, but they must test the same content as typical students. This stipulation continues to be a huge debate topic. Types of alternative assessments include[16] authentic assessment, portfolio assessment, performance based assessment, project based learning, and alternate assessment. Districts object to the inclusion of test scores from students who are disabled in the calculation of whether they are able to achieve AYP or not. They contend that inclusion of such scores in AYP calculations unfairly penalizes districts with larger special needs student populations. Similar debates swirl around the nearly five million students labeled as limited English proficiency (LEP) because some researchers note that tests constructed for native English speaking students are not appropriate for LEP students.[17] Critics charge that No Child Left Behind places an undue burden on districts with higher numbers of students from special populations such as LEP, special education, and economically disadvantaged students who have historically been poor test performers.

The Debate on the Reauthorization of NCLB

The original intent of NCLB enjoys widespread support among lawmakers, civic leaders, and educators. There is no doubt that NCLB has increased attention for the neediest students in our schools. It is the *implementation* of NCLB that draws disapproval. Districts continue to object to the strong federal intervention in their local district policy development. States claim the federal mandates in the current version of NCLB are too constricting and they are calling for more local flexibility by reducing the federal role. Civil Rights leaders however, fear that relaxing NCLB mandates will reduce or eliminate the focus on the students most in need. [18] The general public appears to share this view. In the 42nd Annual Phi Delta Kappa/Gallup Poll, 4 out of 5 Americans feel the state government should be responsible for accountability standards and the federal government should *not* have a role in holding schools accountable. [19] In a September 2011 speech President Obama stated:

And I want to say the goals behind No Child Left Behind were admirable, and President Bush deserves credit for that. Higher standards are the right goal. Accountability is the right goal. Closing the achievement gap is the right goal. And we've got to stay focused on those goals. But experience has taught us that, in it's implementation, No Child Left Behind had some serious flaws that are hurting our children instead of helping them. Teachers too often are being forced to teach to the test. Subjects like history and science have been squeezed out. And in order to avoid having their schools labeled as failures, some states, perversely, have actually had to lower their standards in a race to the bottom instead of a Race to the Top. They don't want to get penalized? Let's make sure that the standards are so low that we're not going to be seen failing to meet them. That makes no sense. So starting today, we'll be giving states more flexibility to meet high standards. Keep in mind, the change we're making is not lowering standards; we're saying we're going to give you more flexibility to meet high standards. We're going to let states, schools and teachers come up with innovative ways to give our children the skills they need to compete for the jobs of the future. Because what works in Rhode Island may not be the same thing that works in Tennessee — but every student should have the same opportunity to learn and grow, no matter what state they live in. [20]

Responding to concerns from the states, the president has added a provision to NCLB that will allow states to apply to relax some portions of NCLB. States wishing to remove specific NCLB mandates must demonstrate they are embarking on "serious state-led efforts to close achievement gaps, promote rigorous accountability, and ensure that all students are on track to graduate ready for college or a career. [21] According to the Federal Department of Education, to relax the mandates in NCLB districts must show that they are:

❑ Transitioning students, teachers, and schools to a system aligned with college and career ready standards;

❑ Developing differentiated accountability systems; and

❑ Developing comprehensive principal and teacher evaluation and support systems.

Currently, 11 states have filed applications to increase state flexibility and 39 states, Washington, DC and Puerto Rico have indicated intent to do the same. There has been a push to reauthorize, or overhaul NCLB since 2007. [22] The opportunity for increased state and district flexibility will provide requested relief for schools. But, even if the state in which you teach has applied for increased flexibility, No Child Left Behind remains a significant component of nearly every school in the United States.

School Choice and NCLB

So, if you are thinking, what does all this mean, and how exactly does it work? Believe me, you are not alone. Even veteran teachers have been known to raise an eyebrow or two because schools may incur consequences each year they fail to meet AYP. As explained earlier in the chapter, if a school fails to meet AYP for two years, parents must be offered the choice of transferring their child to a higher performing school. Districts must provide transportation for students choosing to transfer. In the third year of not meeting AYP schools must offer school choice and supplemental educational services, such as private tutoring. Schools who fail to meet AYP for four consecutive years must offer school choice, supplemental services, and undergo outside corrective actions, such as replacing staff or implementing a new curriculum. In year five schools must offer all the aforementioned in addition to planning a restructuring plan. The school must implement the restructuring plan in year six. Restructuring may include reopening the school as a charter school.

NCLB and The Period of Choice

NCLB's school choice provision offering students the choice to transfer to higher achieving schools is most troubling to high poverty urban districts. The push for school competition to create better performing schools began several decades ago. In 1981, researcher James Coleman reported that students in private and parochial schools were outperforming students in public schools. He cited that non-public schools maintained more rigorous standards, had fewer discipline problems, and produced higher test scores. The Coleman Report drew attention to the philosophy of 1950's economist, Milton Friedman. Friedman had long believed that public schools would be more efficient if they functioned as part of a competitive market, asserting that public schools had little reason to improve because they largely had a captive audience. School choice actually began in the early 1970's as *magnet schools* were created in response to the unpopularity of desegregation busing. Magnet schools are public schools that are academically rigorous and focus on a specific subject such as art, science, or drama. Magnet schools were created in response to bussing and were intended to attract a diverse population of students during a time when schools were trying to become more integrated. They often have selectively competitive entrance standards, and according to some studies, often outperform private and catholic schools. [23]

NCLB reinvigorated the move toward school choice by requiring public schools to offer more options to students attending the failing public schools. Currently, students in public schools have various school choice options open to them other than magnet schools. Such choices include: charter schools, school vouchers, home-schooling, and open enrollment. The issue of school choice is politically charged with much debate and support, both pro and con. The controversy stems from the federal government's use of tax dollars to support children attending non-public schools. Opponents of school choice believe the funding would be better spent to support struggling public schools. They also feel that school choice encourages higher achieving students to seek alternative schools.

School choice supporters argue that alternative schooling is a move in the right direction for several reasons. First, they claim, as Freidman theorized, that public schools will be encouraged to become more effective. Second, school choice advocates believe that students will have the opportunity to attend higher achieving schools. Third, as stipulated in *NCLB*, school choice places parents in the driver's seat with the increased responsibility to make choices in the education of their children. [24] The following chart outlines the school choice options currently available in most school districts.

School Choice Options

Charter schools	Public schools that receive public school funds and are able to operate largely independent of the school district and the school board. [25]
Vouchers	Instead of the public dollars for each pupil being distributed to the school district, parents receive a credit that they can use to pay to whatever school their child chooses to attend, typically a private or parochial school. [25]
Open-Enrollment	Allows a student to attend schools within the district that may not necessarily be the closest neighborhood school. Typically students may attend any school in the district where space is available.
Home-schooling	Students who are taught in the home either exclusively or in conjunction with part-time school attendance. It is estimated that over a million students between the ages of 5 and 17 are home schooled. [26]
Magnet Schools	Public schools designed to draw a diverse population from a larger area and have specially designed themed curriculum such as performing arts, health/science, or technology. [6]

The Good, the Bad, and the Ugly of NCLB Standards and Accountability

Most educators believe in the premise that NCLB will help to increase student achievement through teacher accountability; it is *just* what the doctor ordered. Accountability simply makes sure we are responsible for teaching what is required. However, many educators and researchers alike have expressed dissatisfaction with the implementation, namely the one-time annual test snapshot to evaluate a year of student progress. Like any polarizing issue, equally compelling arguments resound loudly on both sides of the coin. The United States Department of Education boasts that **No Child Left Behind is raising student achievement for millions of children in schools nationwide and is helping to close** the achievement gap **between the highest and lowest achieving students.** [27] As a new teacher, it is essential that you are aware of how this pivotal legislation may affect you in the classroom. Like it or not, student performance on annual assessments has become the marker of success or failure for students, administrators, school districts, and most importantly, teachers. [28] This is not an endorsement of high stakes testing. It is an endorsement of being the best teacher possible in your school system. Whether you agree or not, it is the teachers' responsibility to ensure that the instruction conforms to the standards expected to be taught and tested.

When NCLB was implemented in 2001, schools were given a window of time to prepare for the changes. Most, if not all schools, aligned their district curriculum to the state standards ensuring students are learning the appropriate material for the appropriate grade. Standards-based education is a system that develops curriculum, assessments, and professional development based on educational milestones. Simply put, content standards are clear and measurable statements of exactly what students, pre-K through 12, should know and be able to do at any given moment in time.   States, in turn, adopt and adapt these national standards for their district. Performance standards, on the other hand, assess how well students meet the content standards.

In 2010, the Council of Chief State School Officers (CCSSO) and the National Governors Association Center for Best Practices (NGA Center) led an initiative to develop Common Core Standards in language arts and math for grades K – 12. These college and career readiness standards were developed with the input from a wide range of stakeholders. Common Core Standards were developed to define the knowledge and skills students should gain in their K – 12 education careers to graduate and succeed in entry-level, credit bearing academic college courses and in workforce training programs.[29] These Common Core Standards are:

❑ Aligned with college and work expectations;

❑ Clear, understandable and consistent;

❑ Inclusive of rigorous content and application knowledge through high order skills;

❑ Built upon strengths and lessons of current state standards;

❑ Informed by top-performing countries, so that all students are prepared to succeed in our global economy and society; and

❑ Evidence and/or research based. [29]

It is imperative that duplication teachers new and old stay abreast of the current standards not only for their grade level and subject, but for other grades too. *Content standards* detail exactly what students need to know…which tells what needs to be taught. *Performance standards* detail what students should be able to do, essentially assessing how well students have learned the content standards. The first step will be to align your curriculum to the goals in your content area. Begin by looking at each area (reading, writing, math, science, social studies) and the content and performance standards for which your grade level is responsible. Effectively aligning the curriculum requires a collaborative effort across grade levels. If across grade level collaboration is not possible, meet one-on-one with the teachers that most impact your grade level to discuss and confirm who will be responsible for what learning objectives. This valuable process, called *curriculum mapping,* helps to ensure that no objective goes uncovered and every educator knows for what they are responsible. Curriculum mapping will also help to identify content gaps and eliminate teaching duplication.

Once the curriculum mapping is completed or in process, a scope-and-sequence model can be developed. A *scope-and-sequence model* describes the manner in which the curriculum is organized across grade levels. *Scope* refers to the breadth and depth of the content. *Sequence* refers to the order in which the concepts and skills will be covered over a period of years. Once this process is completed, the material you are responsible for covering will be clear. *Teaching to the test* should no longer be a part of your vernacular. You will no longer be teaching to the test because you will teach using the objectives developed directly from state standards upon which the state assessment is drawn. Your goal as a teacher is to assure that your students have the best tools possible to pass the state achievement tests. *This is the test that your class will pass because you will teach the objectives, that come from the goals, that are drawn from the curriculum, that are based on the standards, that will eventually create questions, that will appear on the test that your class will pass.*

No one, not the federal government, the Supreme Court, the President of the United States, the state government, or even the local school board can tell you *HOW* to teach your content. It's up to you! Your main objective will be to make sure the material is covered according to the scope and sequence. So, if you want to turn a unit on the Civil War into a class movie re-enactment – go right ahead! If you need to go outside in search of pollinating cannabis plants – happy hunting. If you want to assign a supportive reaction paper for a chapter on global warming – go for it!

Be assured that NCLB or its reauthorization will not be the last piece of legislation to come down the pike during your career directing you *what* to teach. It is unlikely that any legislation will ever tell you *how* to teach. A law or act should, never affect your style, your methods, and ultimately your gifts.

So, when you hear other teachers say, "NCLB is telling me how to teach!" Know that this is not necessarily so. Educators who excel in the classroom continue to do so regardless of what laws come and go. That's just what *good* teachers do.

Chapter Activities

1. Using the Ohio Department of Education website, research Local Report Cards for two school districts and identify and compare the various performance measures.

2. Locate and complete a "practice" section of the Ohio Graduation Test in your future teaching discipline. Describe the learning objectives that you believe need to be mastered to successfully pass the test.

3. *No Child Left Behind Debate*. Divide into two groups: one in favor of NCLB and one not in favor of school choice. Research the pros and cons and engage in a student debate on the topic.

4. *School Choice Debate*. Divide into two groups: one in favor of school choice and one not in favor of school choice. Research the pros and cons and engage in a student debate on the topic.

5. Obtain a teacher handbook from a school district. Describe the regulations and/or guidelines that are most likely created to comply with the No Child Left Behind Act of 2001.

6. Obtain a teacher handbook from a school district. Locate the sections that provide guidance for teachers in meeting the goals and objectives for the standards you will be teaching. What additional information do you believe would be helpful for you as a teacher?

Chapter Summary

1. The No Child Left Behind Act of 2001 is a reauthorization of the Elementary and Secondary Education Act of 1965. The ESEA was described as President Johnson's War on Poverty.

2. The ESEA of 1965 and the NCLB Act of 2001 mark the most significant federal intervention in public schools. Both federal Acts seek to establish standards and accountability to reduce achievement gaps between affluent and poverty stricken students.

3. No Child Left Behind stipulated that all children achieve proficiency in reading and math by 2014 and mandated regulations for many components including:

    a. Use of Title I funds

    b. Teacher quality

    c. Curriculum standards

    d. Guidelines for Limited English Proficient students

    e. Annual assessments

    f. Achievement accountability for all students (subgroup accountability)

    g. Rigorous accountability measures

4. As mandated by No Child Left Behind Act of 2001, the state of Ohio established four performance measures:

    a. State Indicators

    b. Performance Index Score

    c. Adequate Yearly Progress

    d. Value Added

5. Most educators strongly believe in the intent of NCLB, but are troubled by the implementation. One point of dissatisfaction is the one-shot assessment high stakes testing stipulation.

6. As stipulated in NCLB, schools not achieving AYP are subject to increasingly invasive consequences such as offering students the option to attend higher achieving schools (school choice options).

7. 1950's economist Milton Freidman was the first to recommend schools operate as a competitive market as a means to improve student achievement, citing the success of private and parochial schools.

8. Many educators believe the NCLB unfairly penalizes students in low-income environments, as it fails to recognize the influence of variables such as parental support and high mobility rate.

Notes

1. United State Department of Education. (2006, February). *National assessment of Title I*. Retrieved from www2.ed.gov/rschstat/eval/disadv/title1interimreport/vol1.pdf.

2. Association for Educational Communications and Technology. (2001). *Elementary and Secondary Act of 1965*. Retrieved from http://www.aect.org/about/history/esea.htm.

3. Wikipedia. (n.d.). *Elementary and Secondary Education Act*. Retrieved from www.en.wikipedia.org/wiki/Elemenary_and_Seconary_Education_Act.

4. United State Department of Education. Institute of Education Sciences (2006, February). *National assessment of Title I* . Retrieved from www2.ed.gov/rschstat/eval/disadv/title1interimreport/vol1.pdf.

5. Brown, A. (2011. August 18). *Americans recognize value of great teachers and college degrees*. Retrieved from www.thequeue.com/2011/08/americans-recognize-value-of-great.html.

6. Kaplan, L. S. & Owings (2011). *American education: Building a common foundation*. Belmont, CA: Wadsworth, Cengage Learning, 158.

7. Great Schools. (n.d.). *No Child Left Behind*. Retrieved from www.greatschools.net/definitions/or/nclb.html.

8. United States Department of Education (2007). *Building on results: A blueprint for strengthening the No Child Left Behind Act*. Retrieved from www.ed.gov.html (¶2).

9. Gelman, J.A., Pullen, P.L. & Kauffman, J.M. (2004). The meaning of highly qualified and a clear road map to accomplishment. *Exceptionality, 12*(4), 195-207.

10. May, J. J. (2006). Role of money, race, and politics in the accountability challenge. *Journal of Urban Learning, Teaching and Research, 2*, 39-47.

11. Ohio Department of Education. (2007). *Highly qualified teacher toolkit school year 2007-2008*. Retrieved from www.ode.state.oh.us/GD/Templates/Pages/ODE/ODEDetail.aspx?Page=3&TopicRelationID=850&Content=30523.

12. Ohio Department of Education. (2007). *Highly qualified teacher toolkit school year 2007-2008*. Retrieved from www.ode.state.oh.us/GD/Templates/Pages/ODE/ODEDetail.aspx?Page=3&TopicRelationID=850&Content=30523.

13. Sunderman, G. L., Tracey, C. A., Kim, J. & Orefield, G. (2004). *Listening to teachers: Classroom realities and No Child Left Behind*. Cambridge, MA: The Civil Rights Project at Harvard University.

14. Smyth, T. S. (2008 January-February). Who is No Child Left Behind leaving behind? *The Clearing House* 81(3). 133-137.

15. McLaughlin, M. J. & Thurlow, M. (2003, September). Educational accountability and students with disabilities. *Educational Policy, 14*(4), 431-451.

16. National School Boards Association. (2011). *NCLB Assessments*. Retrieved from www.nsba.org./School Law/Federal-Regulations/Archive/NCLBAlternativeAssessments.txt.

17. Abedi, J. (2003). The No Child Left Behind Act and English language learners: Assessment and accountability issues. *Educational Researcher*, 33(1), 4-14.

18. Klein, A. (2011, October, 31). *Clock ticking on senate bill to overhaul NCLB*. Retrieved from www.edweek.org/articls/2011/11/02.

19. Bushaw, W. J. & Lopez, S. J. (2010, September). A time for change: The 42nd annual Phi Delta Kappa/Gallop poll of the public's attitudes toward the public schools, *Phi Delta Kappan, 92*(1), 8 – 26.

20. Office of the Press Secretary (2011, September 23). *Remarks by the President on No Child Left Behind Flexibility.* Office of the Press Secretary. Retrieved from www.whitehouse.gov/the-press-office/2011/09/23/remarks-president-no-child-left-behind-flexibility: The White House.

21. Office of the Press Secretary (2011, September 23). *Remarks by the President on No Child Left Behind Flexibility.* Office of the Press Secretary. Retrieved from www.whitehouse.gov/the-press-office/2011/09/23/remarks-president-no-child-left-behind-flexibility: The White House.

22. U.S. Department of Education (2011, November 15). *11 states seek flexibility from NCLB to drive education reforms in first round of requests.* Retrieved from www.ed.gov/news/press-releases/11-states-seek-flexibility-nclb-drive-education-reforms-first-round-requests.

23. Sadker, M.P. & Sadker, D. M. (2005) *Teachers school and society*. (7th ed.). Boston: McGraw Hill, (p.244).

24. Morrison, G, (2009). *Teaching in America*. Boston, MA: Allyn and Bacon. (p. 375).

25. Hall, G. E., Quinn, L. F. & Gollnick, D. M. (2008*). The joy of teaching*. Boston, MA: Pearson Education, p 177.

26. Koch, J. (2009). *So you want to be a teacher*. Boston, MA: Houghton-Mifflin.

27. Elementary and Secondary Education Act Reauthorization (2009, December). *Talking Points.* Lawyers Committee for Civil Rights Under Law. Retrieved from www.nces.ed.gov/programs/digest/d09/ch 2.asp.

28. Ward, M.J., Montague, N. & Linton, T.H. (2003). Including students with disabilities and achieving accountability: Educators' emerging challenge as cited in Cassandra Cole (2006, Fall). *Closing the achievement gap series: Part III What is the impact of NCLB on the inclusion of students with disabilities?* Center for Evaluation and Educational Policy 4(11), 1-11. (p. 1).

29. National Governors Association Center (2010, March 10). *Common core standards initiative.* Retrieved from www.corestandares.org.

8

THE 21ST CENTURY CLASSROOM

Jennifer Wancata teaches kindergarten for the Chicago Public Schools and this is her story.

It is fair to say that I am the girl from the country. Growing up in a little town about an hour south of Cleveland, Ohio, I was used to cornfields, cows, and Carhartts. After high school, I decided to attend a college that was in the middle of the cornfield. I experienced the same small town feeling, just like back home, where things were comfortable and consistent and people looked just like me. One day while student teaching, I decided that I wanted to experience a teaching position that would be different from everything I knew, something new, something far away from my life in the cornfields. I decided then and there that I was going to seek a teaching job in "the city."

Just weeks after graduation, a fellow classmate and I packed up and moved to Chicago, the third largest city in America, and I was in the middle of it, with only my country experience behind me. I quickly landed a job on the city's south side in the Englewood neighborhood. To say that I experienced culture shock would be an understatement. I will never forget my first day, wondering how I ended up there. Was this really what I wanted to do?

As I walked into my first classroom, I realized my four years of study in college had only told part of the story. The kids were in uniforms, there were no yellow school busses, kindergartners walked to school alone, police stopped by to make sure all was calm, and it seemed everyone received a free lunch. It all seemed so chaotic compared to my hometown roots. It took me awhile to adjust to teaching. It was the complete opposite of everything that I ever knew.

Now nearly five years later…the halls aren't so chaotic, the uniforms are a sign of student pride, kindergartners are uniquely capable individuals, police are a sign of support, and students receive free lunches because they are truly poverty-stricken. I have learned that "my kids" are just like the others, they love and care just like other kids, and they have parents that care just as much. Yes, this really was what I wanted to do.

MOST, if not all, college preparatory programs require coursework on multicultural education. This chapter presents an overview of issues and concepts for consideration in that first teaching assignment. There are hundreds of books discussing multicultural education in public schools, and you are encouraged to further your reading on the topic. A list of popular authors is provided at the end of the chapter.

Multicultural education, for the purposes of this book, refers to creating a classroom that is accepting, respectful, and validating for *all* students—from students who are cognitively and physically challenged, to students who are economically disadvantaged, to students who are non-English speakers. The subsequent two chapters focus on student populations that have proven most challenging for novice teachers.

You may ask yourself why this information is necessary. The fact of the matter is that Jennifer's case story represents a vast majority of new teachers. Many are born and raised in communities that are largely white and homogenous and attend colleges that mirror that background. Graduates seeking to teach in districts resembling their hometowns may not find positions available. A novice teacher may turn to a district where, on the first day, he or she may gaze upon a sea of faces that do not mirror his or her own. In the same way, it is also possible for the same scenario to occur to a minority teacher entering the workforce.

Just the Facts

The National Center for Education Statistics reports that nearly 84% of all teachers in the United States are white females, and 87% of teachers in large towns and the urban fringes are also white. Coupled with the fact that about 40% of all students in public schools are students of color[1], it is conceivable that the potential for miscommunication exists.

It seems that everyday, there is an article revealing the growing number of people of color in the United States. Gollnick and Chin estimate that by 2020, students of color will approach 50% in the nation's classrooms.[2] Currently, about 43% of the population consider themselves to be part of a racial or ethnic group.[3] The U.S. Census Bureau reports that growth in the Hispanic population has surpassed African Americans and will continue to grow,[4] comprising an estimated 40% of the 2030 population.[5] Asian American comprise roughly 4% of the population, but are currently the fastest growing ethnic group the country[6] The chart below proposes what we can expect the student landscape to exhibit in 2010.

Student Population Estimates in 2010	
White, Non-Hispanic	50%
Hispanic/Latino	20%
African American	14%
Asian/Pacific Islander	4%
American Indian	1.5%
Alaskan Native	

Source: U.S. Census Bureau 2006[6]

Defining Diversity

When we think of school diversity, we often conjure up pictures of black and white. In truth, diversity encompasses a vast spectrum of differences where race is only part of the story. All school populations, including rural and suburban, have tremendous student diversity. In addition to race, students come to school with an array of characteristics. Some of those differences may include socio-economic status, exceptional abilities or challenges, native languages, ethnicity, and sexual orientation. The diversity umbrella brings with it assorted cultures and learning styles.

RACIAL DIFFERENCES

Common Frames of Reference

Defining common terminology is important to ensure a shared understanding of terms. Race refers to people bound by common biological traits such as color of skin and texture of hair, whereas ethnicity refers to the country of ancestry origin.[7] Unlike in the past, it is now commonly acceptable to claim membership in more than one group, typically referred to as multi-racial.

Culture is defined by society's rules of acceptable behavior, including values, mores, and beliefs. These shared common behaviors generate a "norm" by which we are guided, and that norm is based on the behaviors of the dominant societal group. In the United States, the dominant group is characterized as white, heterosexual, Christian, English-speaking, middle-class, able bodied and male.[8] Membership in the dominant group for some, affords a sense of cultural superiority referred to as *Ethnocentrism.* Individuals not belonging to the dominant group often feel the need to conform to the dominant culture's value system to be socially accepted or economically successful. Our culture is a socially transmitted phenomenon learned from the family unit through a process called *Enculturation,* as well as from the larger society, through a process call *Acculturation.*

If we recall the "unspoken rules" that governed our households, we can distinguish how and where we learned many of our behavioral patterns. These behavior patterns were learned from sources such as parents, friends, as well as media. We are all strongly socialized by media influences such as television, internet, family, and life events. From all of these experiences, we develop a lifetime of "experiential tapes" that govern how we behave. Where did they come from? Are they facts or myths? How many of the following have you heard?

"Don't go outside with your hair wet."

"Spicy foods will make you sick."

"If you drink coffee, it'll give you liver spots and stunt your growth."

"Don't go swimming until at least an hour after you eat."

"Your hair will grow back thicker if you shave it."

Prejudice, Discrimination, and Racism

These "tapes" may be true or false. Regardless, they settle in our heads as things we "know." We are governed in much the same way with the stereotypes we have grown up hearing. We can all recall stereotypes we heard at home that we now know to be a fallacy or at best, only half the story. Stereotypes are sweeping generalizations applied to all members of a group that ignore individual differences.[9] Such labels may result in prejudices that lead to discriminatory behavior. Prejudice is a cultural attitude formed from negative stereotypes. Discrimination is acting negatively based upon those prejudices. Racism is introduced to the equation when one has beliefs of cultural superiority *and* the power to act on those beliefs to the detriment of another. Racism is prejudice and discrimination paired with power.

Race Matters

Discussions of race are difficult because of the deep emotions attached to the subject. These discussions are essential for new teachers because these issues strongly affect classroom interaction. Simply put, racism is a belief that certain ethnic groups are inherently superior and more *capable*. This belief is problematic and is compounded when accepted and entrenched in one institutional core of America, including our schools. Fortunately, many Americans do not share racist beliefs but that does not alter the fact that it exists. Institutional racism is defined as systematic policies and practices that have the effect of disadvantaging certain racial or ethnic groups.[10]

Examples of such institutional practices include:

- ❑ exclusionary housing practices
- ❑ bank lending policies
- ❑ racial profiling by security and law enforcement workers
- ❑ the under- and mis-representation of certain racial groups in the media
- ❑ lack of positive images of some racial groups
- ❑ excessive negative representation
- ❑ barriers to employment for certain groups
- ❑ professional promotion based on ethnicity
- ❑ differential access to goods and services

❑ lack of services in largely minority neighborhoods

❑ lack of appropriate shopping access in largely minority neighborhoods

❑ opportunities to belong to certain clubs and organizations

❑ academic placements based on ethnicity

It is understandable that many find it difficult to believe such practices exist. Covert or quiet racial discrimination practices are so commonplace that we do not notice them. Shirley Chisholm, the nation's first African American congresswoman, remarked that racism is so universal in this country, so widespread and deep-seated that it is invisible because it is so normal.[11]

Deficit Theory, the Classroom and You

So why does all this matter? It matters because as humans, our belief systems govern our behavior, and in the case of a teacher, our personal philosophies guide how we approach teaching in the classroom. If one believes that his or her culture and/or race are inherently superior, then what follows is that other cultures must be inherently inferior. The Deficit Theory supposes that some students do poorly in school because they lack the cultural patterns of the dominant culture. Variances in language, social patterns, family structures, and values are perceived as deficits instead of mere differences. This affects students in the classroom because teacher *expectations* are lower for students with perceived cultural deficits. The Deficit Theory is a cyclical pattern that becomes a self-fulfilling prophesy. A teacher whose philosophy includes the Deficit Theory will teach less to students perceived to have cultural deficits. The students in turn, underachieve, and their lack of achievement may be blamed on their cultural deficits. The students' perceived lack of ability relieves the teachers and schools from responsibility since the students are not capable of achievement. Research continues to demonstrate that if teachers expect less, they get less.

Achievement Gap

Maximizing the achievement of all children continues to be a challenge in the United States. Historically, minority students have scored lower on standardized tests. There are multiple theories as to why the disparity exists:

❑ Minorities are more likely to be poor and attend schools with inferior buildings and resources [12]

❑ Minorities are more likely to be placed in lower learning tracks where they receive less instruction and achieve at lower levels [13]

❑ Students who come from different cultural and language backgrounds may be unfamiliar with the norms and values of the dominant group and experience adjustment barriers that may prevent the maximization of instruction [14]

❑ Standardized tests are created based on the experiences of the dominant group; experiences that may not be shared by other cultures

❑ Students from lower socioeconomic levels often enter school without a solid grasp of standard English usage and must spend time learning the language while their peers are immersed in the actual learning processes[15]

❑ Students who are not accepted socially have difficultly focusing on achievement

❑ Educators often perceive a lack of experiences' as a 'lack of intelligence' and assume that a culturally different student is not able to learn

❑ Educators who operate under the Deficit Theory may not perceive the benefits of high level instruction for certain cultural groups

GEOGRAPHICAL DIFFERENCES

Rural, suburban, and urban school populations vary according to demographic characteristics. Rural is defined as communities with populations less than 5000.[16] The state of Ohio has nearly 400,000 rural students, the highest number of any state.[17] Suburban schools border large cities and are often populated by families seeking to escape the difficulties associated with larger cities. Ethnically diverse, suburban students tend to come from moderate to high-income families. Urban schools are those where 75% of the households are located in the central city and are typically populated with lower-income students .[18] With geographical differences, often come grave cultural differences. Rural areas, like urban areas, may be populated with students who are financially poor, but rich in culture. Rural schools tend to place importance on core subjects with the addition of vocational agriculture, home economics, or industrial education to meet student interests. [19] Suburban schools focus more on college preparatory courses,[20] and urban centers offer a wide variety of courses geared toward a diverse student population.

Each type of school organization shares many of the same challenges, but each also faces issues central to the type of school. For new teachers, it is imperative that time is taken to learn and understand the community and culture to make sure it is the best fit for you as the educator.

SOCIAL CLASS DIFFERENCES

Socioeconomic status (SES) is defined by the income level of the family. Schools use family income to determine free and reduced lunch eligibility. Nearly one in every five students under the age of 18 is living in poverty[21] This is a pivotal concept, as socio-economic status, not race, is the most influential factor in the academic and social success of students. Statistically, the number of whites in poverty exceeds Latinos and African Americans,[22] but because the poverty line, those lines appear to be racially drawn.

Poverty, nevertheless, does not occur in isolation. The Annie E. Casey Foundation labels a child at-risk if living with four of the following factors: [23]

❑ Family does not have health care

❑ Family is led by a single parent

❑ Head of the household is unemployed

❑ Family is living in poverty

❑ Head of household is not a high school graduate

❑ Family is receiving welfare benefits

Poverty Matters

Educationally, poverty can have a devastating effect on the academic achievement of students. Morrison [13] writes that:

❑ Students of poverty have less access to the nation's best schools because the best schools are located in wealthier locations where poor students do not reside

❑ Students of poverty are more likely to attend school in inadequate buildings

❑ Students of poverty are more likely to attend schools lacking appropriate educational materials

❑ Students of poverty are more likely to be placed in lower track academic classes based on their SES level

❑ Teachers of lower track academic classes spend less time in direct instruction with students

❑ Teachers of lower track academic classes may use less effective teaching strategies

❑ Teachers view students in lower track academic classes negatively [13]

Further, children of poverty are less likely to receive adequate health care, dental care and proper nutrition and experience a greater incidence of vision, hearing, and asthma problems.[25]

LIMITED ENGLISH DIFFERENCES

Nearly 51% of all public schools in the United States have students who are Limited English Proficient.[1] Over the last twenty-five years, the number of students speaking a language other than English has increased from three to nine million with Spanish being the most widely spoken.[26] The Ohio Department of Education describes four widely accepted approaches to teaching students with Limited English Proficiency.

❑ Bilingual Education is based on the notion that students are more likely to learn if they understand what is being taught, and they will not fall behind their English-speaking peers if they are able to continue learning subject matter in their native language.

❑ In the Immersion Approach, non-English speaking students are instructed in English only. While instruction is to be tailored to the cognitive level of the learner, they are often 'sink or swim' programs that expect non-English speaking students to succeed by submersing them in English speaking classrooms. Immersion programs, considered traditional approaches, are not widely successful.

❑ English as a Second Language Programs (ESL) are "pull-out" English classes and are adapted to the specific English proficiency level of the learner. In Ohio, ESL programs are used as the main program in conjunction with native language support services.

❑ In-class Inclusion Instruction Programs also called Transitional Methods, use the students' native language as a medium of instruction to learn other subjects with their English speaking peers. English instruction increases as the skill level increases until English is used exclusively.

❑ Individual Tutoring is used when there are very few non-English speaking students. Tutors may be trained or volunteers working under a trained professional.

The first United States law providing funds to establish programs assisting students in learning English was the Bilingual Education Act of 1968. In 1973, the Comprehensive Bilingual Education Act provided training for teachers and the necessary funds for purchasing materials. While not mandating bilingual education, the 1974 landmark case Lau v. Nichol did specify that special bilingual programs with understandable English instruction must be available to non-English speaking students.[28]

Growth and success of bilingual education programs in the United States has been marginal, and controversy surrounds how to best instruct non-English speaking students. There are hundreds of different languages spoken by millions of students. The learning curve is compounded when the language barrier includes racial and ethnic differences as well.[29] Bilingual education has its share of controversy. Some believe that bilingual education threatens English as a "unifying bond that preserves our common culture"[30] , and English should be the only language spoken in schools. This notion has produced an English-only trend and the legality of such a movement is still under consideration. Bilingual education supporters believe that the English-only movement promotes a lack of tolerance for other cultures and is a form of discrimination. An increase in English-only legislation has sparked a reduction in bilingual funding. This discussion is a pivotal one as the dropout rate for Limited English Proficient Hispanic students is nearly 50%.[31]

Morrison offers a summary of current research on students learning English as a second language. First, Morrison notes that students learn English at a faster rate using the Transitional Method where their native language is used for instruction. This is especially significant for at-risk students. Secondly, students can acquire a second language at any age, but the skill is maximized in early childhood. Thirdly, students who are proficient in their native language and have a solid academic background will be more efficient in their newly acquired language.[32]

Jacquelyn May teaches secondary history and economics at Prepa Tec Valle Alto of Tecnologico de Monterrey Nuevo Leon, Mexico and this is her story.

While I graduated with a minor in Spanish, I didn't really expect to use it. After all, my major was International Business and I was ready to conquer the business world. Well, in case you have been asleep for the last year.....businesses are not really looking for recent grads who know nothing beyond their economics textbook. So, I was in the right place (Mexico) at the right time (July) and before I knew it I was standing in the middle of a classroom (August) teaching history to students who were learning English as a second language (Yikes!). But not only was I supposed to teach English in an immersion program, I was supposed to be preparing them for college in the United States! (Yea, right!)

Ok, I told myself that people (like me) who teach English as a second language are talented, gifted people equipped with a natural sense of patience (I may have been wrong on several counts here). My first eye-opening encounter occurred when I realized I was in a linguistic nightmare. After teaching my first lesson and collecting the first homework assignment, I found myself struggling to read a host of made up words between English and Spanish (Spanglish) as well as sentences without verbs, and other essential parts of speech.

"He Russia Better Make" I recall an answer to a quiz about Peter the Great.

I quickly discovered I had a whole new objective. I had to overcome the fact that my students' first language was Spanish, not English. This may sound like a "duh" statement, but there is a great difference between speaking Spanish and teaching Spanish.

Frustrated and kinda scared I began grading for grammatical errors instead of content. But I knew that was not going to work. I had to teach them history—in English. This is where the light bulb went on. The students were brilliant, but being in their first semester of high school, in an exclusive ESL program, history was going to be a very difficult subject to master.

The first two weeks were an uphill battle, but I soon realized I had to alter my teaching style. I began to use what could be called a four-pronged approach. I paired my class presentations with readings, detailed descriptions, pictures, and translations. I hoped this would help them understand, retain, and actually write out concepts. It was absolutely amazing watching my students evolve right before my eyes. All they needed was more than one way to get the information. Incredibly simple. Some weeks they would understand and be able to apply more than 100 new words to a concept. One of the most memorable challenges was teaching the concept of "feudalism." Having my students learn and master this concept was very difficult, but also very rewarding. Now, I have earned the right to call myself a teacher!

TEACHING ALL STUDENTS

Regardless of the language spoken, skin color, culture difference, or ability level, kids are just kids. As a trained educator you are capable of success in any classroom, but the following paragraphs may offer some helpful recommendations.

First and foremost, establish a positive learning environment by having high expectations for *all* students. As noted earlier in the chapter, students may come to your classroom from a variety of backgrounds and situations, of which you will likely have little control. However, you can control your classroom, your attitudes, your prejudices, your depth of care, and opportunities you provide for students to succeed. Creating classrooms where ALL have the same opportunities is a thoughtful and conscious process. Take time to examine your personal philosophy and how those beliefs may influence your instructional practices.

Do you believe that all students can excel in the classroom? Or do you believe down deep that some students, perhaps because of their cultural backgrounds, are not as capable of achieving to the same level as their peers? A lack of enriching experiences, typical to students living in poverty, does not translate to lack of ability or intelligence. Your students will look to you as a "truth machine", and your words have the power to build up and empower or the destructive force to tear down and destroy in an instant. Acknowledging, reflecting, re-valuating, and re-tooling your personal biases will aid in creating a classroom where all students have an opportunity to succeed.

The following summarizes classroom recommendations from the experts. Sadker and Sadker suggest the following classroom behaviors for teachers. [33]

- ❏ Model skills and behaviors that reflect sensitivity

- ❏ Use classroom strategies that build on individual student learning styles

- ❏ Equalize instructional attention; research suggests that white males receive more active attention than females and minorities

- ❏ Monitor discipline behaviors; teachers discipline boys more often and more harshly

- ❏ Encourage cooperative rather than competitive classroom strategies

❏ Refrain from stereotyping students

❏ Familiarize yourself with different students' backgrounds to better understand their world view (eye contact, touching, personal space, and the extent of your role in the education process)

❏ Avoid segregated seating patterns or activities (boys and girls; minority groupings)

❏ Rotate seating to encourage participation for all students; more attention is typically paid to students sitting in the first two rows

❏ Call on all students and provide appropriate "wait time" for responses; students are often called on more frequently if they are expected to answer quickly and correctly

❏ Provide positive feedback to all students; teachers provide positive feedback to boys more often than girls/minorities

❏ Promote collaborative education rather than individual competition

❏ Monitor your classroom for equitable visual displays. If the walls could speak, what would they say relative to women, people of color, etc?

❏ Assign tasks NOT based on gender biases or racial stereotypes (asking boys to tackle physical or math related tasks and girls for lighter less cognitive tasks)

❏ Encourage open communication between students.

Morrison adds that educators should: [34]

❏ Maintain consistent, relevant, and reciprocal communication with parents

❏ Allow time for students to engage in the language of their choice for informal periods

❏ Help students gain a positive self-esteem by demonstrating their value as individuals

❏ Assume that all your students are capable of achieving at optimum levels

❏ Maximize academic learning time through carefully planned lessons

❏ Reduce "wasted" class time by establishing high expectations for appropriate behavior

❏ Create lessons with ample opportunities for critical-thinking skills

❑ Model and expect a zero-tolerance policy for cultural, linguistic, and ability bias (name calling, racial remarks, and exclusionary practices)

❑ Teach appropriate conflict mediation strategies

Koch recommends the following when working with non-English speaking students: [35]

❑ Speak clearly and at a slower rate

❑ Use gestures and facial expressions

❑ Utilize concrete materials and visuals

❑ Avoid idiomatic expressions that are central to English

❑ Pair English-challenged speakers with peers who are more proficient in both English and Spanish when possible

Transforming your classroom into a multicultural one and offering opportunities for all students to learn in an atmosphere of respect and acceptance is not a difficult one. Nonetheless, it requires deliberate and thoughtful curricular decisions. First, teachers must have a sincere affection for students and the profession of teaching. Secondly, take an interest in the challenges your students face, but those challenges must *take a back seat* to academic achievement. The Deficit Theory has no place in a successful classroom. Students must not fail because they are poor or minority or non-English speaking; with your guidance, they must achieve in spite of it. Sadker and Sadker suggest enlisting a peer to observe you in the classroom to assure that you are interacting substantively with different students in the classroom.[36]

Multicultural Education

The goal of multicultural education is to help transform the classroom so that male and female students, students from different social classes, exceptional students, students with alternative sexual orientations, culturally diverse students, as well as those from the dominant culture all have an equal opportunity to learn.[37] In the following paragraphs Banks and McIntosh [38] present a 5-stage continuum of multicultural education.

CREATING A CULTURALLY COMPETENT CLASSROOM

STAGE 1: *Curriculum of the Mainstream* assumes that the teacher utilizes material presented from a Eurocentric and male-centric view. This approach does not include the voices and experiences of non-dominant groups. According to Banks, this approach may have negative consequences because it "reinforces the dominant groups' false sense of superiority, and denies any opportunity to benefit from the knowledge, perspectives, and frames of references gained from studying and experiencing other cultures and groups".

STAGE 2: *Heroes and Holidays,* also called the *Tourist Approach* is characterized by intermittent bulletin boards and isolated celebrations focusing of food, costumes, music and special celebrations. While it is a step beyond *Curriculum in the Mainstream,* this curriculum is a "sidebar" or an "after-thought" to the REAL curriculum and therefore is not perceived as an integral part of the "real stuff." Further, the Tourist Approach serves to diminish the actual contributions of certain groups by removing them from the "real story."

STAGE 3: *Integration* is an approach where teachers take additional steps to move beyond heroes and holidays to include significant information and curricula about groups beyond the dominant group. Banks notes that this material is still added to the REAL curriculum, which continues to be presented from a male-centric, Eurocentric view. Examples of this stage, according to Banks, include adding books written by authors of color or by women or developing a unit covering, for instance, the important role of women in World War I.

STAGE 4: *Structural Reform* is a stage that moves the instruction to another level because the voices and experiences of non-dominant groups are "seamlessly woven" into the REAL curriculum providing a more accurate portrayal of their roles. The teacher endeavors continually to examine new perspectives through a variety of lenses.

STAGE 5: *Multicultural, Social Action and Awareness* stage builds on the structural reform stage and adds current social issues such as racism, sexism, and classism in the REAL curriculum. Banks notes that the textbook is but one source in many, including other types of media.

The decision on how you instruct in your classroom will ultimately be yours to make. Nevertheless, it is the responsibility of each educator to create classrooms where all students have the opportunity to succeed.

EXCEPTIONAL DIFFERENCES

Twelve percent of the student population in the United States is currently being educated using an Individual Education Plan *(IEP),* and 26% of those students are currently served in the general classroom for the entire school day.[39] The next chapter provides a brief overview of working with populations that are considered exceptional.

Chapter Activities

1. View Frontline's *A Class Divided (1985)* video and discuss the classroom implications of Jane Elliot's experiment *(60 minutes)*.

2. Enculturation, Acculturation, and the Parent Tapes. In small groups, generate a list of "parent tapes" that you remember hearing as you grew up. Decide whether they are true or false, stereotypes or fact.

3. Thinking back to your elementary and secondary schools days, identify what multicultural education approaches were utilized by your teachers? What changes, if any, may have helped to create a more inclusive environment.

4. View *Children of a Lesser God (1986)* movie and consider Jim Leeds' instructional approaches relative to the following topics *(119 minutes)*.

    a. How we define intelligence

    b. Illustrating a shared culture

    c. Incorporating diverse learning styles and multiple intelligences

    d. Similarities between the challenges faced by students who are deaf and students who are non-English speakers

Suggested Reading:

1. *The pedagogy of the oppressed* (1970) by Pablo Freire

2. *In a different voice* (1982) by Carol Gilligan

3. *Language, culture, and teaching: Critical perspective for a new century* (2001) by Sonia Nieto

4. *Latino Students in American Schools* (2001) by Guadalupe Valdes

5. *Making choices for multicultural education: Five approaches to race class and gender* by (1994) Carl Grant and Christine Sleeter

6. *Multi-ethnic education: Theory and Practice* (1994) by James Banks

7. *Savage Inequalities: Children in America's schools* (1991) by Jonathan Kozol

8. *White Privilege: Unpacking the invisible knapsack* (1988) by Peggy McIntosh

    Available online at http://www.nymbp.org/reference/WhitePrivilege.pdf

9. *Other people's children: Cultural conflict in the classroom* (1995) by Lisa Delpit

Chapter Summary

1. Student diversity extends far beyond race and ethnicity and may also include differences in geography, economics, language, and culture.

2. Creating a culturally competent classroom begins with the examination and identification of "experiential tapes" that may lead to operating under the Deficit Theory.

3. It is essential that teachers maintain high expectations for the success of all students.

4. Multicultural classrooms offer opportunities for all students to learn in an atmosphere of respect and acceptance.

5. Teachers should be aware of and engage in strategies proven to promote academic and social success of all students.

Notes

1. National Center for Education Statistics (2007). *Characteristics of schools, districts, teachers, principals, and school libraries in the United States' schools and staffing survey.* US Department of Education, Washington, DC: U.S. Government Printing Office.

2. Gollnick, D., & Chinn, P. (2002). *Multicultural education in a pluralistic society* (6th ed.). Columbus, OH: Merrill/Prentice Hall, p. 49.

3. Koch, J. (2009). *So you want to be a teacher.* Boston, MA: Houghton-Mifflin.

4. U.S. Census Bureau. (2006) *Statistical Abstract of the United States: 2006* (125th ed.). Washington, DC: US Government Printing Office as cited in G. Hall, L. Quinn and D. Gollnick (2008) The joy of teaching. Boston, MA: Pearson Education, p. 49.

5. Sadker, M. P. & Sadker, D. M. (2005). *Teachers, schools, and society.* (7th ed.). Boston: McGraw Hill, p. 244.

6. U.S. Census Bureau (2006). *Statistical Abstract of the United States: 2006* (125th ed.). Washington, DC: US Government Printing Office as cited in G. Hall, L. Quinn and D. Gollnick (2008). The joy of teaching. Boston, MA: Pearson Education, p. 49.

7. Hall, G. E., Quinn, L. F. & Gollnick, D. M. (2008). *The joy of teaching.* Boston, MA: Pearson Education, p. 177.

8. Ibid., p. 51.

9. Sadker, M. P. & Sadker, D. M. (2005). *Teachers, schools, and society*, (7th ed.). Boston: McGraw Hill, p. 46.

10. Wikopedia: The free encyclopedia. Retrieved from http://en.wikipedia.org/wiki/Institutional_racism.

11. May, J.J. (2006). The role of money, race, and politics in the accountability challenge. *Journal of Urban Learning, teaching and Research*, (2) p. 39 - 47.

12. Commission on the reorganization of secondary education (1918). Cardinal principles of secondary education (Bulletin 1918). Washington, DC: U.S. Department of the Interior (pp. 12-13) as cited in G. Morrison, *Teaching in America*. Boston: Allyn and Bacon, p. 375.

13. Morrison, G.(2003). *Teaching in America*. Boston: Allyn and Bacon, p. 122.

14. Ibid., p. 123.

15. Ibid., p. 124.

16. Debertin, D. L. & Goetz, S. J. (1994). *Differences in rural and urban schools: Issues for policymakers*. Retrieved from http:// www.uky.edu/Ag/AgEcon/pubs/res_other/schlurvr.pdf

17. Morrison, G. (2003). *Teaching in America*. Boston: Allyn and Bacon, p.108.

18. Ibid., p. 109.

19. American Legislative Exchange Council. (1993). The report card on American education. Washington, DC as cited in G. Morrison, *Teaching in America*. Boston: Allyn and Bacon, p. 108.

20. Morrison, G.(2003). *Teaching in America*. Boston: Allyn and Bacon, p. 109.

21. Annie E. Casey Foundation 2006 as cited in J. Koch, (2009). *So you want to be a teacher*. Boston, MA: Houghton-Mifflin, p. 134.

22. Hall, G. E., Quinn, L. F. & Gollnick, D. M. (2008) *The joy of teaching*. Boston, MA: Pearson Education, p. 62-63.

23. Annie E. Casey Foundation 2003 as cited in J. Koch, (2009). *So you want to be a teacher*. Boston, MA: Houghton-Mifflin, p. 136.

24. Morrison, G. (2003). *Teaching in America*. Boston: Allyn and Bacon, p. 121.

25. Hall, G. E., Quinn, L. F & Gollnick, D. M. (2008) *The joy of teaching*. Boston, MA: Pearson Education, p. 65.

26. Koch, J. (2009). *So you want to be a teacher*. Boston, MA: Houghton-Mifflin, p.127.

27. Ohio Department of Education (2008). Characteristics of programs serving LEP students in Ohio. Retrieved from http:// www.ode.

state.oh.us/gd/templates/ pages/ODE/ ODEPrinterFriendlyPage. aspx?Page=3&TopicRelation

28. Morrison, G. (2003). *Teaching in America.* Boston: Allyn and Bacon, p. 137.

29. Sadker, M. P. & Sadker, D. M. (2005). *Teachers, schools, and society.* (7th ed.) Boston: McGraw Hill, p. 54.

30. Sadker, M. P. & Sadker, D. M. (2005). *Teachers, schools, and society.* (7th ed.) Boston: McGraw Hill, p. *55.*

31. Ibid., p. 56.

32. Sadker, M. P. & Sadker, D. M. (2005). *Teachers, schools, and society.* (7th ed.) Boston: McGraw Hill, p. 456.

33. Morrison, G. (2003). *Teaching in America.* Boston: Allyn and Bacon, p. 147-148.

34. Koch, J. (2009). *So you want to be a teacher.* Boston, MA: Houghton-Mifflin, p. 129-130.

35. Sadker, M. P. & Sadker, D. M. (2005). *Teachers, schools, and society.* (7th ed.) Boston: McGraw Hill, p. 478.

36. Banks, J. Multicultural education: Characteristics and goals in Mira and David Sadker (2005). *Teachers, schools, and society.(7th* ed.) Boston: McGraw Hill, p. 49.

37. Banks, J. (1993). Approaches to multicultural curriculum reform. In J. Banks and C. Banks (Eds.), *Multicultural education: Issues and perspectives.* Boston: Allyn & Bacon. and McIntosh, P. (2000). Interactive phases of personal and curricular re-vision with regard to race. In G. Shin and P. Gorski (Eds.), *Multicultural resource series: Professional development for educators.* (p.195). Washington, D.C.: National Education Association. Retrieved from http:// www.mhhe.com/socscience/_education/multi/curriculum/stepds.html.

38. National Center for Education Statistics (2007).*Characteristics of schools, districts, teachers, principals, and school libraries in the United States' schools and staffing survey.* US Department of Education, Washington, DC. US Government Printing Office.

THE INCLUSIVE CLASSROOM

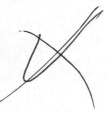

Judy Jackson May served as a teacher of students with multiple disabilities from 1983-1996.

When I walked into my first classroom nearly twenty-five years ago, I knew it was the beginning of something very special. I had not planned to become a special education teacher but was hooked after serving part of my student teaching experience in a Multiple Handicapped Unit (now called Multiple Disabilities). Training to become a speech and language clinician, my time in the unit was the most exciting and rewarding experience imaginable. I returned to school to earn my Master's Degree so that I could teach students with multiple disabilities. For more than a decade, I worked with students who had a wide range of abilities such as: Down Syndrome, Spina Bifida, Autism, Orthopedic Impairments, Cerebral Palsy, Developmental Delay, blindness, and profound deafness.

In the early years, my students and I were the only ones in a self-contained classroom. We were not a "real" part of the school community. I learned the depths of love that flows reciprocally from student to teacher. I witnessed the parent heartbreak that comes with parenting a child with multiple disabilities. I felt the unfortunate ignorance of those who did not see the magnificent abilities in our classroom. I tired of the endless struggle for resources for kids perceived not to be worthy. And I painfully watched students who wanted to sit at the lunch table and be just like "the other kids."

By the time I left the classroom, fortunately tremendous changes had been realized. Our classroom was in the front hallway of the school, the students spent significant time in the general classroom, they proudly walked the hallways free of stares, parents spoke to them just as they did other students, we received instructional materials just like other classes, and they did sit at the lunch table...just like the other kids.

THE 21ST Century Classroom chapter provided an overview of student diversity in the classroom. This chapter extends the discussion to another group of students considered exceptional learners. Exceptional learners are students falling outside the range of typical learners. The range of exceptional learners covers a continuum from students with severe physical and cognitive impairments to students who are considered gifted. Exceptional learners, especially those with physical and cognitive disabilities, have been subject to decades of disappointing and unbecoming attitudes on the part of the school community. In the past, these attitudes led to inadequate educational services, lack of school support and acceptance, and exclusionary educational and social practices. Legal intervention and parent advocacy over the last thirty-five years has provided educational safeguards, but the struggle for social acceptance still exists. This chapter provides a brief overview of working with populations considered "exceptional."

STUDENTS WITH DISABILITIES

As noted in the previous chapter 12% or over 6 million students in the United States are currently educated using an Individual Education Plan (IEP), and 26% of those students are currently served in the general classroom for the entire school day.[1] The following table represents the disability categories for the 6,109,600 students served in the United States.[2]

Disability	Numbers Served	Percentage
Specific Learning Disabilities	2,780,200	45.5
Speech or Language Impairments	1,157,200	18.9
Cognitive Disability	545,500	8.9
Emotional Disturbance	472,400	7.7
Multiple Disabilities	133,900	2.2
Hearing Impairments	72,400	1.1
Orthopedic Impairments	63,100	1
Other Health Impairments	561,000	9.1
Visual Impairments	26,000	.4
Autism	193,600	3.1
Deaf and Blind	1,600	.1
Traumatic Brain Injury	23,500	.3

The Ohio Department of Education defines each disability as follows.[3]

Specific Learning Disability means a disorder in one or more of the basic psychological processes involved in understanding or using language, spoken or written, that may impede the ability to listen, think, speak, read, write, spell, or do mathematical calculations.

Speech or Language Impairment means a communication disorder, such as stuttering, impaired articulation, a language impairment, or a voice impairment, that adversely affects a child's educational performance.

Cognitive Disability (replaces mental retardation) means significantly below-average general intellectual functioning, along with deficits in adaptive behavior, manifested during the developmental period that adversely affects a child's educational performance.

Emotional Disturbance means a condition exhibiting one or more of the following characteristics over a long period of time and to a marked degree, that adversely affects a child's educational performance:

a. An inability to learn that cannot be explained by intellectual, sensory, or health factors.

b. An inability to build or maintain satisfactory interpersonal relationships with peers or teachers.

c. Inappropriate types of behavior or feelings under normal circumstances.

d. A general pervasive mood of unhappiness or depression.

e. A tendency to develop physical symptoms or fears associated with personal or school problems.

Multiple Disabilities means simultaneous impairments (such as cognitive disability- blindness, cognitive disability -orthopedic impairment, etc.), the combination which causes such severe educational needs that they cannot be accommodated in Special Education programs solely for one of the impairments.

Hearing Impairments means an impairment in hearing, whether permanent or fluctuating, that adversely affects a child's educational performance, but is not included under the definition of deafness.

Orthopedic Impairment means a severe orthopedic impairment that adversely affects a child's educational performance. The term includes impairments caused by congenital anomaly, impairments caused by disease (e.g., Poliomyelitis, bone tuberculosis, etc.), and impairments from other causes (e.g., cerebral palsy, amputations, and fractures or burns that cause contractures).

Other Health Impairment means having limited strength, vitality, or alertness, including a heightened sensitivity to environmental stimuli that results in limited alertness with respect to the educational environment, that adversely affects a child's educational performance.

Visual Impairments means an impairment in vision, including blindness, and even with correction, adversely affects a child's educational performance.

Autism is a developmental disability (generally evident before age three) significantly affecting verbal and nonverbal communication and social interaction, that adversely affects a child's educational performance. Other characteristics often associated with autism are engagement in repetitive activities and stereotyped movements, resistance to environmental change or change in daily routines and unusual responses to sensory experiences.

Deaf-Blindness means simultaneous hearing and visual impairments, the combination which causes such severe communication and other developmental and educational needs that they cannot be accommodated in special education programs solely for children with deafness or children with blindness.

Traumatic Brain Injury means an acquired injury to the brain caused by an external physical force or by other medical conditions, including but not limited to: stroke, anoxia, infectious disease, aneurysm, brain tumors, and neurological insults resulting from medical or surgical treatments. The injury results in total or partial functional disability or psychosocial impairment or both, that adversely affects a child's educational performance.

Deafness means a hearing impairment that is so severe that the child is impaired in processing linguistic information through hearing, with or without amplification, that adversely affects a child's educational performance.

LEGAL PATH TO SERVICES FOR STUDENTS WITH DISABILITIES (1972-2008)

Two Seminal Cases

Two major cases in 1972, *Pennsylvania Association for Retarded Citizens (PARC) v. Pennsylvania* and *Mills v. Board of Education,* drew national attention to the plight of students with disabilities. The *Pennsylvania Association for Retarded Citizens v. Pennsylvania* case found that the State Board of Education and thirteen school districts violated its statue of publicly supported education and the 14th Amendment rights of the students by denying students with mental retardation equal educational opportunities. The results of the *PARC* case established four points:

1. All students with mental retardation are capable of benefiting from an education/training program.

2. Education cannot be denied for students with disabilities.

3. The State undertook the provision of educating all children and could not deny students with mental retardation access to free public education and training.

4. Preschoolers with disabilities cannot be denied access to preschool programs for children without disabilities. The court further established students with mental retardation between the ages of six and twenty-one should have access to free public education and should be educated in the same programs as their peers without disabilities.[5]

In the District of Columbia's *Mills v. Board of Education* case, the parents of seven children excluded from school, sued the school board for violating the 14th Amendment. The results of this seminal case found the students' exclusion unconstitutional and established procedural safeguards for due process, labeling requirements, and placement and exclusionary criteria for students with disabilities.[5] These cases led to the enactment of The Education for All Handicapped Act and Operating Standards for Educational Agencies Serving Children with Disabilities.

In 1975, the United States Congress enacted the Education for All Handicapped Children Act (EHA) (Public Law 94-142) which stipulated that all public schools receiving federal funds must provide an appropriate education to children with physical and mental disabilities. This pivotal Act established the *Six Pillars of Special Education.*[4]

1. The **zero reject** pillar states that no child with a disability can be denied a free appropriate public education.

2. The **least-restrictive environment** (LRE) pillar ensures that students with disabilities cannot be segregated from their peers. LRE states that students must be educated with their non-disabled peers to the maximum extent possible.

3. The third pillar, **the individual education program** (IEP), is a document that is designed for each child and specifies his or her educational plan, services rendered, procedures required, the responsible parties, and the resources allocated.

4. The **procedural due process** pillar establishes safeguards and rights for students and parents. These rights include the 'right to records confidentiality', the right to examine all records, the right to receive written notification (in native language) of changes to educational placement or classification, the right to an impartial hearing in the event of a disagreement regarding educational plans, and the right to legal representation.

5. The fifth pillar, **nondiscriminatory assessment**, protects the evaluation process of students with disabilities. Students must be evaluated by a multidisciplinary team with evaluation tools that are not racially, culturally, or linguistically biased.

6. The final pillar is to ensure **significant parent participation** in all the decision-making processes that affects the child's education.

The Education for All Handicapped Children Act was revised and renamed the Individuals with Disabilities Act (IDEA) in 1990. IDEA was subsequently amended in 1997 and 2004, adding modifications to better serve students with disabilities.

On July 1, 2008, the *Ohio Department of Education released Operating Standards for Educational Agencies Serving Children with Disabilities.*[6] The purpose of the standards is to align the Individuals with Disabilities Act of 2004 and the No Child Left Behind Act of 2001. The new operating standards emphasize high expectations and must include the timely intervention of services.   Highly qualified teachers must learn flexibility in evaluating student progress, and exceptional students are encouraged to have instruction with the general curriculum and partake in school activities with their non-disabled peers as much as possible. These goals help to serve as a transition into life after high school.

Individualize Education Program

The IEP is a written document reviewed annually that stipulates the student's educational plan and must include:

1.   current level of performance

2.   measurable academic and functional goals

3.   how the goals will be measured

4.   the related services to be provided to meet the goals

5.   the extent that the student will participate with nondisabled peers

6.   any accommodation required to measure achievement on state assessments

7.   the duration of services

8.   transition services and postsecondary goals

STUDENTS WITH DISABILITIES IN THE CLASSROOM

Mainstreaming, Inclusion, and Full-inclusion

Prior to the Education for All Handicapped Children Act of 1975, students with disabilities were sadly educated in self-contained classrooms nearly out of sight of their non-disabled peers. Following the 1975 landmark EHA legislation, students were **mainstreamed** into the general classroom or "natural" environment for selected activities reserving the self-contained classroom as their "homebase." Morrison defines the natural environment as the least restrictive environment, or where the child would attend if they did not have a disability.[7] In the mainstreaming model, students with disabilities are educated away from their non-disabled peers for much of the day and are not real "members" of the natural environment. The Special Education teacher is responsible for the majority of the academic instruction, and students who are disabled must "earn" their way to a substantial role in the natural environment.

Today, many students with disabilities are educated in **inclusionary** models with the natural environment as their "homebase." This model supposes that the natural environment is a "right" and not a "privilege." Inclusion assumes the natural environment as the least restrictive environment where the majority of instruction is delivered. Students may be "pulled out" for instruction with a variety of specialists, but remain part of the natural environment. **Full inclusion** differs from the inclusionary model in that all services are delivered in the natural environment and separate classrooms are not available.

Natural Environment Instruction

Forty-five percent of students with IEP's are students with learning disabilities participating in inclusion or full inclusion. The fact of the matter is that the education of students with disabilities is the responsibility of all teachers. Research shows that students with disabilities educated in inclusive classrooms show academic gains on standardized tests, with on-task behavior, and with the motivation to learn. [8] Additionally, inclusive classrooms generally do not have a negative impact on the academic performance of students without disabilities.[9]

Most educators favor inclusion philosophically, but due to a lack of training, may be somewhat uncomfortable teaching students with disabilities. This is a valid concern and not overlooked by educators and policymakers. Schools have support personnel to assist in instruction and service delivery as mandated by law. Support personnel include speech-language pathologists, occupational and physical therapists, adaptive physical education teachers, reading specialists, special education teachers, counselors, psychologists, paraprofessionals, administrative staff, and other teachers.

An instructional strategy promoting the success of students with disabilities does not differ greatly from those for non-disabled students. Teachers should: maintain high academic/social expectations, refrain from ability grouping, use peer coaching, promote a sense of belonging in the classroom, be open to learning new skill-sets, maintain a positive attitude, and make the most of available services. Collaboration and consultation is key in the development of appropriate instruction for students with disabilities. Specialists and experts in the field of special education can provide insights to alternative teaching strategies not previously considered. Modifications and adjustments will likely benefit all students. Differentiated instruction, the practice of using a variety of instructional strategies to address different learning needs of students, is essential.[10]

Tomlinson (as cited in Koch) [11] discusses fundamental concepts relative to differentiated instruction:

❑ Students differ in their interests, learning styles, experiences, life circumstances, and readiness to learn.

❑ Student differences are significant enough to make a major impact on what students need to learn, the pace at which they need to learn, and the support needed from teachers and support staff to learn it well.

❑   Students learn best when supportive adults push them slightly beyond where they can work without assistance.

❑   Students learn best when they can make a connection between the curriculum, their interests and life experiences.

❑   Students learn best when learning opportunities are natural.

❑   Students are more effective learners when classrooms and schools create a sense of community in which students feel significant and respected.

❑   The central job of schools is to maximize the capacity of each student.

First full sentence: Morrison suggests consideration of the following points when creating an inclusive classroom.[12]

❑   Assess the individual learning needs of all students and determine which needs require special attention and accommodation.

❑   Determine which special needs can be met without assistance and which will require outside collaboration and consultation.

❑   Determine any special training that may be necessary.

❑   Determine the instructional accommodations necessary for individual students.

❑   Determine the environmental accommodations necessary for individual students.

❑   Determine what must be done to ensure students are accepting and helpful toward students with disabilities.

A positive classroom culture and climate cannot be overstated. Teachers are vital role models in the classroom, and non-disabled students will emulate the attitudes modeled by their teachers, negative and positive.

GIFTED AND TALENTED

According to the National Association of Gifted Children (NAGC), students are considered gifted if they show evidence of high achievement capability: intellectual, creative, artistic, or leadership capacity. Gifted and talented learners are entitled to services not ordinarily provided by the school and are afforded activities to better develop these capabilities.[14]

The NAGC estimates that approximately 6% of the student population is academically gifted. Considerations for students with exceptional talents are often overshadowed by the concerns of students with disabilities. Students who are gifted and talented typically perform above their peers on a number of levels, but may also face challenges such as boredom, negative peer pressure,[15] isolation, loneliness, pressure to achieve, and fear of failure, and may even contemplate suicide. [16] Gifted learners are typically served in the natural environment, and teachers should be aware of these social and academic challenges.

Programs for the gifted and talented learner are not consistent between schools and/or districts. Quality programs sometimes remain a challenge for schools struggling to meet the academic needs of all students. The curriculum is not typically altered, but is presented in an accelerated format or through enrichment programs. [17] Increased opportunities exist for secondary students through advanced placement courses, post-secondary options, and accelerated academies.

INTERVENTION ASSISTANCE

Many schools establish intervention assistance programs or teams for teachers requesting support for students with exceptionalities in the classroom. Procedures for requesting student assistance vary from school to school, so it is important to be familiar with teacher and administrative expectations. The team of educators assigned to assist in the process will require adequate documentation of target behaviors. Methodical and objective documentation of student target behaviors over an appropriate period of time is essential to provide a baseline for subsequent intervention. The team may also request a written plan for classroom strategies the teacher currently has in place.

Students with disabilities are students first and disabled second. Educators should focus on student abilities and not dwell on the disabilities. Consideration for the talents and abilities of all students in the classroom will provide the best guide in meeting the needs of exceptional learners in the natural environment.

Chapter Activities

1. Observe a natural classroom environment and describe the differential instructional techniques employed.

2. Choose one of the disabilities below and discuss possible approaches to intervention and classroom instructional and environmental modifications.

    a. A kindergarten child with a mild hearing deficit who attended preschool for two years. (female)

    b. Second grade student is in a temporary cast from a broken leg. (female)

    c. Third grade student who is non-communicative and does not work well with peers, demonstrates a slight expressive language delay, and appears to enjoy adult company. (male)

    d.   Popular ninth grade student on a 4.2 reading level, 6.5 math level that is an excellent piano player, and has parents who are very concerned about his progress. (male)

    e.   Senior student who has taken the State Graduation test several times and has not yet passed. (female)

3.   Describe the steps you would employ to discover the learning styles of your students: elementary, middle and high school.

4.   Using one of the scenarios from question 2, provide examples of the type of documented data required to assist in planning intervention strategies. How would you collect it?

5.   Using one of the scenarios from question 2, create an Individual Education Plan (IEP) using the first five required components.

Chapter Summary

1.   All teachers are responsible for the education of students with disabilities.

2.   Two pivotal cases are responsible for drawing needed attention to creating equitable learning environments for students with disabilities.

3.   The *Education for All Handicapped Act of 1975* later renamed the *Individuals with Disabilities Act of 2004* outlines the 6 pillars of special education.

4.   The Individual Educational Program is a legal written document stipulating the students' education plan, services required, necessary accommodations, measurable goals, and the service duration.

5.   Teachers should maintain high academic and social expectations, refrain from ability grouping, promote a sense of belonging, be open to learning new skill-sets, and maintain a positive attitude.

Notes

1.   National Center for Education Statistics (2007). *Characteristics of schools, districts, teachers, principals, and school libraries in the United States' schools and staffing survey.* US Department of Education. Washington, DC. US Government Printing Office.

2.   U.S. Department of Education (2005). Office of Special Education Programs Data Analysis System. Retrieved from http://www.census.gov/compendia/statab/tables/08s0255.xls

3.	Ohio Department of Education (2008). *Operating standards for Ohio educational agencies serving children with disabilities.* Retrieved from http:// www.ode.state.oh.us/GD/Templates/ Pages/ODE/ODEDetail.aspx?page=3& TopicRelationI D=968& ContentI D=28143&Content=60076 (p.16-19).

4.	Hill, P. D. (2008). *An examination of the impact of IEP team composition and transition planning upon the success of students with cognitive disabilities in urban schools.* Unpublished doctoral dissertation, Bowling Green State University- Bowling Green, Ohio

5.	Yell, M.L (2006). *The law and special education* (2nd ed.). Upper Saddle River, NJ: Pearson Education, Inc as cited in P. D. Hill (2008) Ibid.

6.	Ohio Department of Education (2008). *Operating standards for Ohio educational agencies serving children with disabilities.* Retrieved from http://www. ode.state.oh.us/GD/Templates/ Pages/ODE/ODEDetail.aspx?page=3&To picRelationID=968 &ContentID =28143&Content=60076 (p.16-19).

7.	Morrison, G.S. (2003). *Teaching in America.* (3rd ed.). Boston, MA: Pearson Education, Inc. (p.167).

8.	National Center for Education Restructuring and Inclusion (1995) as cited in K. Whitbread (n.d.). What does the research say about inclusive education? Retrieved from http:// www.wrightsla.com/phprint.php

9.	York, J., Vandercook, T., MacDonald, C., Heise-Neff, C. and Caughey, E.(1992). Feedback from teachers and classmates about integrating middle school learners with severe disabilities in regular classes. *Exceptional Children*, 58(3), 244-259 as cited in K. Whitbread (n.d.). What does there search say about inclusive education? Retrieved from http://www.wrightsla. com/phprint.php

10.	Koch, J. (2009). *So you want to be a teacher.* Boston, MA: Houghton Mifflin Co. (p.164).

11.	Tomlinson, C. (2000). Reconcilable differences? Standards-based teaching and differentiation. *Educational Leadership*, 58(1), 6-11 as cited in J. Koch(2009). So you want to be a teacher. Boston, MA: Houghton Mifflin Co.(p.165).

12.	(p. 165)

13.	Morrison, G.S. (2003). *Teaching in America.* (3rd ed.). Boston, MA: Pearson Education, Inc. (p.177).

14.	National Association of Gifted Children Retrieved from http://www.nagc. org/

15.	Feldhusen, J. F. (1998, June). Programs for the gifted few or talent development for the many? *Phi Delta Kappan*, 79 (10), 735-38 in M. P.Sadker

& D.M. Sadker (2005). Teachers, Schools, and Society, (7th ed.).Boston, MA: McGraw Hill (p.65)

16. Galbraith, J. (1989, May). Gifted youth and self-concept. Gifted youth and self-concept. *Gifted Education*, 15(2), 15-17. in M. P. Sadker & D.M. Sadker (2005). Teachers, Schools, and Society, (7th ed.). Boston, MA: McGraw Hill (p.66)

17. Koch, J. (2009). *So you want to be a teacher*. Boston, MA: Houghton Mifflin Co. (p.164).

Index